A ...ventures
with Brad Leone,

star of
Bon Appétit's
hit video series
It's Alive

Brad Leone was born and raised in the woods of rural northern New Jersey. The fields, forests, rivers, and shores of the Northeast have been his playground since he was a kid. They're also where he finds incredible ingredients to cook with and turn into signature fermentations. Inspiration comes from all around: hikes, trips to the dock, campfires when it's cold, and hanging out poolside in the heat of summer.

Field Notes for Food Adventure follows Brad through a year of journeys to his favorite destinations, showing you how to find and cook with the food that makes each place special. Brad taps maple trees for syrup, forages for ramps and mushrooms, pulls up baskets full of blue crabs, and teaches you about fermentation and why you should eat more squid and seaweed. Each chapter brings you on an excursion and delivers ingenious recipes you can make at home, always with a Leone twist.

Many recipes are super simple, like Sumac "Lemonade," Maple-Pecan Sweet Potatoes, or Steak and Shrooms with Saucy Sauce. Others are fun projects, like Fermented Chile Hot Sauce, Spicy Smoked Tomato Chicken, or Squid Pizza (made with Brad's Sourdough). And of course there's a Big Stock, Fermented Garlic Maple Syrup, and a few "Spoon Sauces." You'll also pick up some of Brad's favorite spice blends, seasonings, and condiments, like Fermented Pepper Paste, Spicy Mustard made from scratch, and Fermented Tartar Sauce.

This is a book about experimentation, adventure, fermentation, fire, and having fun. And hey, you might just learn a thing or two while you're cooking.

Recipes and Stories from the
Woods to the Ocean

Field Notes
for Food
Adventure

Brad Leone

Photographs by Pat O'Malley

Voracious

Little, Brown and Company
New York   Boston   London

Stonington, Connecticut, September. Gutting fish with my dad and Kenyon, who caught his first fish while working on this book.

I dedicate this book to PeggyMarie
and our two sons, Griffen and Callen

Wild brown trout, caught
with fly rod

Contents

Blue Hill Bay, Maine, Summer.
Living my best life.

Field
Notes
for
Food
Adventure

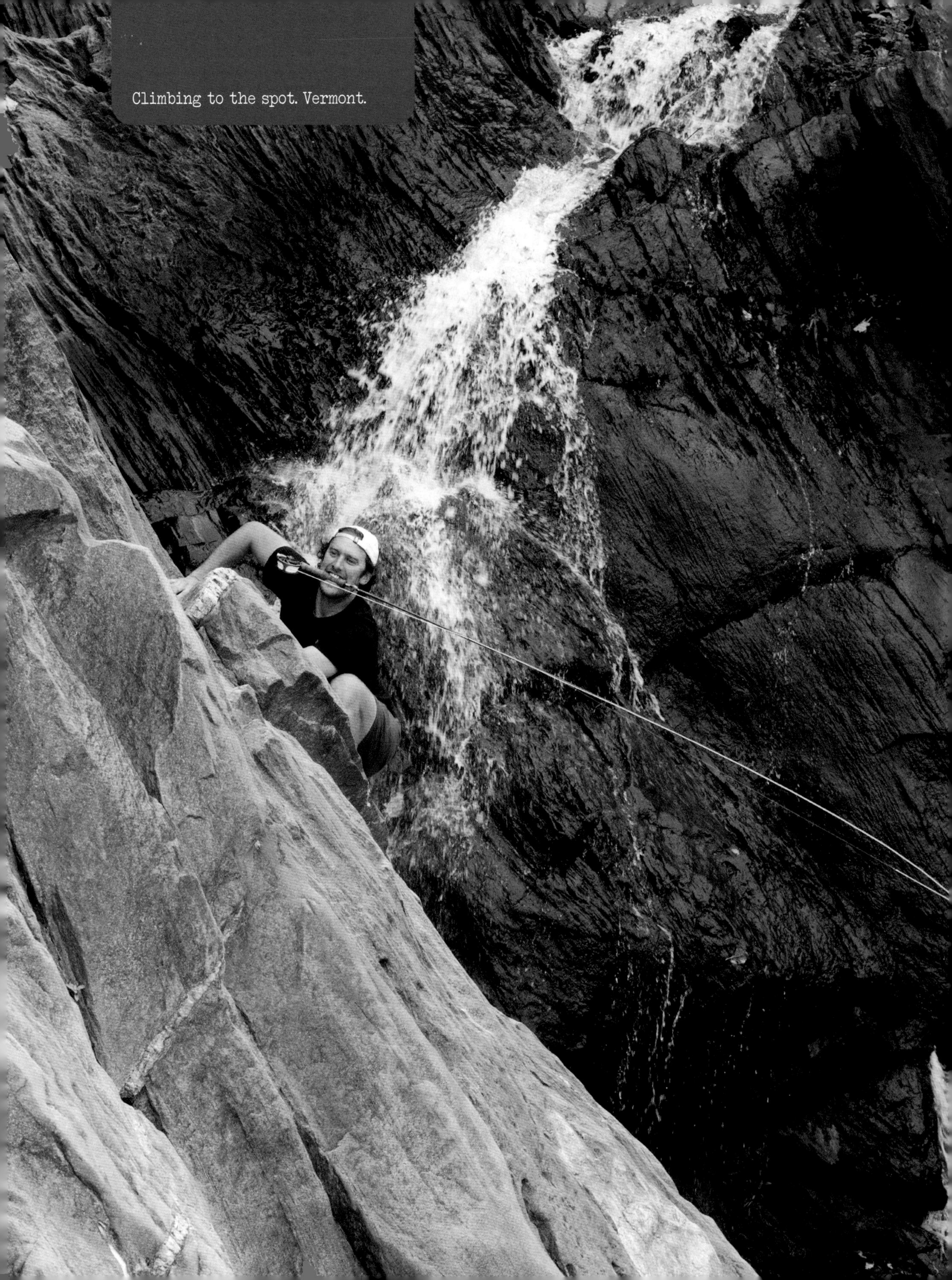

Climbing to the spot. Vermont.

Introduction
Field Notes

When I tell people I'm from New Jersey, people always think of an industrial wasteland across from New York City, with shipping containers and warehouses as far as the eye can see. But that's not the part of Jersey I mean. I grew up an hour or two north of the industrial zones. Once you leave the cities behind, the sights turn from industrial to suburban—but don't stop there. Soon the houses and strip malls turn into forests and lakes.

Living in and around New York City for years made this a very familiar trip. My parents still live in the house I grew up in, and it's this wooded part of northern Jersey that helped shape me into the person I am. I love the whole east coast of the US, and specifically the northeast, with its cold waters, old Appalachian mountains, and road trips north to Maine, Connecticut, New York, and Vermont. I love how the Northeast is affected by all four seasons. Sure, it's always sunny and nice in California but summer all year sounds kind of terrible to me. Call me crazy, but I need that change and all the great things that follow with it. It reminds me that I'm alive and a part of this mystery we call life.

This book is a set of stories, notes, recipes, and ideas from a year following those seasons in the Northeast, visiting some of my favorite places, getting closer to where our food comes from, and doing some of my favorite activities outdoors. No matter what time of year it is, there's always something extraordinary happening if you know where to look.

We start in spring, when the world brings new life from the cold winter. Produce peeks out from the cold ground. Maple sap starts to flow and certain mushrooms, fish, and birds come into season. Everything is excited to be alive, fighting to flourish—and that includes me.

Next, we roll into 96% humidity and the hot season we call summer. Fruits and veggies come to market with big variety. We go "down the shore," have barbecues, and spend time at waterholes to cool off. This is when I eat lighter; the season becomes a part of you.

Then autumn shows its beautiful face. My favorite season! The leaves start turning all of the colors—there's a reason people travel from all over the world to

Vermont, outside Burlington

experience the autumn here. It's unbelievably beautiful. The light in the sky changes and the days start getting shorter and cooler. The produce is amazing, deer season is approaching, crabbing and fishing are on fire. It's the best.

And finally old man winter rolls in, and I couldn't be happier. Sure, the weather makes life harder in some ways, like getting to work in the snow or shoveling walkways, but you either get into it or move to Florida. I grew up stacking wood, shoveling snow, raking leaves, and mowing the grass. Did I hate it in the moment? Sure. But looking back, I'm glad I learned what it's all about: working hard to play harder. The change in seasons builds character.

Grif and his tomatoes

A proper crab table

Life is not a fairy tale, but it sure as hell seems to be what you make of it. It's the experiences you have alone and with others. Throughout this book I share some of the ones I've had over the course of this year. It's a journey of food, pictures, and stories—some of the ways I live and cook. It's about getting your hands dirty and getting involved in food not just as fuel and nutrition, but as a universal language of love and humanity.

Get lost in the pictures and stories. I hope they inspire you to get out there and have your own experiences. Use these recipes exactly as I've written them, or riff on them to make them your own. You may notice that I don't love giving exact cook times, and instead prefer to tell you how you'll know it's

done. Same thing with certain seasonings: ultimately, you are the judge. Take control and experiment, and you'll learn something. Part of becoming a good cook is learning to trust your instincts and senses more than a recipe that was written by someone using slightly different tools and ingredients.

Whatever you do with this book, HAVE FUN doing it. Even if my "job" didn't involve cooking (and I've had a lot of different jobs that didn't) food is an essential part of life. I can't hide how happy it makes me to cook and eat with people. Like each season, life's just too damn short.

All the food in this book starts with season and a particular place. The food came from real life—what we cooked and ate and preserved from each trip we took to my favorite spots in the northeast. My buddy Pat and his photo assistant Kenyon joined me on every trip (which we undertook with plenty of covid-19 precautions), and we had some times out in the wilderness that I'll remember forever. I'm so grateful to have spent this time with them, and all the other characters we met on our journeys.

While I hope you do get the urge to make this food and get out into nature in your own neck of the woods—whether that's New Mexico, North Dakota, or New Hampshire—remember to be safe when you do so. Take care of the natural world—leave it better than you found it, it's the only one we've got. And know that cooking over live fire, experimenting with fermentation, foraging for and catching your own food, all come with their own risks. People have been doing these things for thousands of years, but it's still possible to screw up and harm yourself or others. Follow simple safety tips and act at your own risk.

So cook, explore, take notes, daydream, laugh, cry. Experience whatever emotions come to you. I share these pages with the intent to inspire. Love is the light. — *Brad*

Cruisin'

Mighty Maple

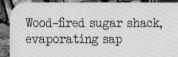

Wood-fired sugar shack,
evaporating sap

1

Maple syrup and its journey from tree to table are well associated with the Northeast. Imagine snow-covered cabins with smoke billowing from small chimneys, mountains of pine dotted with naked birches, covered bridges, roadside sugar shacks, and pancakes on the griddle.

When it comes to maple syrup, many of us have a longstanding breakfast relationship with the condiment, and that might be it. I grew up with frozen waffles and generic grocery store syrup on the door of my mom's fridge. Maple syrup (in one form or another) certainly is a North American mainstay, on the table at every breakfast joint or diner and generously applied to breakfast food nationwide. The sweet flavor is unique and a perfect addition to your morning routine.

Did you know that maple flavor is often imitated and much of the breakfast syrup found on grocery store shelves varies greatly in quality and authenticity? From loose (but kinda thick), mostly sweet, watered down corn syrup with food coloring (with only a little shot of real maple in it) to the "real deal" small batch stuff that comes straight from the tree, you can really geek out on syrup.

These days people are spending more money on quality ingredients, splurging on high-end olive oil and fancy vinegars, but may not be as quick to spend $25 and up on maple syrup. My advice: if you can spend more, you should. When you taste the real stuff, it's like what they write children's books about…it's a candy from Mother Nature.

People have harvested and consumed maple sap and syrup for generations. Nowadays, modern producers have their own rigs to produce this tree candy; from big companies to small families and hobbyists tapping trees from New Jersey to Maine, and beyond. I know many folks working hard to gather the sap and boil it down. It's a ritual, a family tradition, and a business. I'm a huge fan either way. The syrup industry yields over $300 million in global annual sales.

Vermont and Canada get a lot of attention for their maple syrup production, and rightfully so. Vermont produces 42% of the US supply, while Quebec accounts for 70% of the entire global supply. There are plenty of turf wars up north with some strong feelings and pride around whose syrup is best. But knowing what pure maple syrup really is, and what it takes to make it… that is hugely underrated.

I knew a little about maple syrup production, but wanted to learn more firsthand. I initially made some plans locally to learn the process, but it was a weird winter and a strange spring. The weather was all over the place and the plan fell through. It happens, and it was right on theme with this year…Gotta be flexible right? Things happen outside of your control and you adapt to them. Luckily, a good friend put me in touch with a different sugar-shack legend, John C. Stockin, and the weather improved. We ran into some prime sap-collecting conditions and were able to hook up with John in the beautiful Catskill region of New York. John is old school and boils in wood-fired shacks, which he's been running for decades. I learned a lot: thanks, John, for your teachings.

Preparation:

There's only a small window to actually make maple syrup. As with so many good things, much work occurs beforehand. Tons of hours are needed to prepare, regardless of whether your setup is big or small. You need to clean the lines that deliver sap from the trees, along with the tanks that hold it, and split and stack cords of firewood—all while hoping Mother Nature will stay on your side. The prep work is a headache to try to plan around because nature doesn't consider your ideal personal timeline.

The sap pump

The Mighty Maple:

The right trees can produce 15-20 gallons of sap every year. But the production of sap depends on many variables including climate, rainfall, heat, and seasonal change. As a result, sap production can be fickle and the end product amount can be unpredictable from season to season.

Tapping the Trees:

Maple sap is the sugar water that trees create and feed on. You drill or tap holes into different types and sizes of maple, then collect the sap that flows out. This takes time and patience—even at the height of the sap's flow, it is just a trickle.

Boiling:

Buckets of sap get heaved into a space with a hot stove, where the sap is boiled down. Some folks use propane to boil down the sap, but a lot of folks still use wood as the fuel source. Some believe gas can give off-flavors to the syrup and that wood fire is just always better. Doing anything with wood fire makes it harder to control and maintain consistency, but no one said this was easy! The real art to making syrup is in the boiling: years of intuition and experience lead sugar shack operators to dial in the temperature and color of the syrup.

Syrup!

This is the result of the art of boiling: a very thick, very sweet, perfectly colored syrup. All of those features can vary farm to farm and in a good way. And after all the work it takes to get to this point, I don't ever want to hear that the good stuff is too expensive. You really get what you pay for.

The final product ready to be chilled

Seeing how syrup is made with people who not only produce great product, but really care about the environment and community, was incredible. As I left John and Javi at the sugar shack that night, the memory of the fire stuck in my head. The heat and steam made the shack sweat as the giant oven glowed hot in the night, like an old steam engine, as the sap boiled down. That image and the sweet smell of evaporating maple sap will always be with me.

The photo boys and I left with a few bottles of maple syrup, but gained much more than that. The experience left me oddly inspired to be a better person. I couldn't wait to get home to share this liquid gold with my family, hoping one day, maybe, to tap my own trees.

Don't end your relationship with maple syrup at the breakfast counter. Processed/bleached sugar isn't so great and having healthier alternatives is important. I love honey and agave. Now, I often grab the maple instead! Give it a try. Maple syrup is much more than a pancake condiment, it should be a main ingredient in your kitchen.

Shrimp and Sap Soup

Note: There are many kinds of soy sauce—some made entirely of soy, others including wheat—made in different styles depending on the culture and tradition they come from. I prefer Japanese shoyu, which is made with wheat as well as soy, so that's what I turn to for this and most other recipes that call for soy sauce.

This is a really fun way to cook with tree saps—which provide a slight earthy sweetness. Maple is just one of the many saps you can consume and mess around with. Birch trees also provide a tasty sap! If you don't have access to sap, this recipe works great with water and a little splash of maple syrup too—experiment with what works for your taste. This is a satisfying soup that can be eaten at any time of the day.

Peel and clean the shrimp, reserving the shells and heads. Refrigerate the shrimp.

In a medium saucepan, one you'd make soup in, add a little oil and brown the shrimp shells and heads over medium-high heat for a few minutes. Remove and reserve the shells. Add the onions and mushrooms and let them brown and caramelize for a few minutes. Add the garlic, chile, and ginger.

Add the sap and soy sauce to the pan. Return the shrimp shells to the pan and allow the broth to simmer and reduce down for about 30 minutes. I reduce it just until the liquid gets a touch sweet and spicy and has depth. The sap has naturally occurring sugars in it. If reduced for longer, the sap would turn into the lovely syrup we like so much.

Once the broth is how you want it, strain out the solids. Add the shrimp and simmer for a few minutes until the shrimp are perfectly cooked, opaque throughout.

Meanwhile, in a separate pot, cook your noodles of choice according to the package directions. Divide the noodles between bowls and ladle the soup over them. Garnish with radishes and scallion.

10 to 12	large shrimp, shells and heads on canola oil
5	pearl onions, halved
1/2 cup	maitake (hen of the woods) mushrooms
1	shiitake mushroom, sliced
2	garlic cloves, sliced
1/2	Fresno chile, sliced into rings
1 tsp.	grated fresh ginger
6 cups	maple sap (or water with a splash of maple syrup)
1/4 cup	soy sauce (I used shoyu)
	rice noodles or other long noodles
3	radishes, sliced
1	scallion, sliced

Maple - Pecan Sweet Potatoes

Serves 6

I have nostalgia in my heart for sweet potatoes. My mom made them every week, along with meatloaf. Everyone likes them, from kids to old cranky people—kind of like maple syrup.

Sweet potatoes do have a little natural sweetness, but they're also quite earthy and savory. Maple syrup highlights those flavors, but even with the nuts and butter, this does not come across as a dessert. It could be a simple vegetarian meal or a side dish to something like roasted monkfish tail. Go ahead and load it up with other stuff—what's great about sweet potatoes is their versatility.

People freak about how long to cook steak or potatoes, but listen, we're not building a rocket engine here. If your potatoes aren't cooked through at 40 minutes, let 'em go for longer. They're done once a cake tester pushes easily through them.

6	small sweet potatoes
4 Tbsps.	salted butter
1 cup	pecans, chopped
2 Tbsps.	maple syrup
Pinch	cinnamon
1	cardamom pod
1/3 cup	sour cream
1/2 tsp.	lemon juice
	kosher salt and ground black pepper
	chives, sliced (optional)

Preheat the oven to 375°F. Wrap the potatoes in foil with a little bit of water trapped inside. Place on a sheet pan or directly on the oven rack and bake until soft and liquid begins to caramelize in the foil. This will take a good 40 minutes or more depending on the potato.

In a small saucepan, melt the butter and add the pecans, allowing them to get toasty and bloom in the butter for a couple minutes. Add the maple, cinnamon, and cardamom. Cook over low heat until the nuts are loosely glazed.

Mix together the sour cream and lemon juice. Season with salt and some pepper.

Split the roasted potatoes and spoon the pecan mixture over them. Spoon a little sour cream mixture on top. Sprinkling on some chives wouldn't hurt you.

At first look it's hard to tell what's going on here. These blue tubes are made of plastic and plug into small taps that are drilled into the tree's softer wood, where the sap travels freely. A large production like this can take up acres of land and have miles of tubing, which feeds into a large collector. Every day the sap must be transferred to larger tanks at the sugar shack. Here, the sap waits to be boiled down to syrup. Maple trees that are managed for sap production tend to be most active in the spring. There is a small window of time for this entire syrup-making process to begin with, but then, narrowing the timeline further, warm days and cold nights are best for sap draining. Conditions matter!

Sugar shack operators like John and Javi
spend weeks collecting sap and boiling
it down. The smell in the shack is really
something. Anyone who loves maple should
try to experience it. Lots of shacks like
John's are open and friendly to visitors who
want to stop and see the show.

You can really get into it. Load the
car up and drive around to hit a bunch
of shacks during maple season. It's good,
clean fun, and you'll meet some interesting
characters along the way. Every producer's
syrup is slightly different, and discovering
those nuances becomes its own delight, like
tasting wines.

Note: Salting meat ahead of time is one of
the most important things you can do to
it. It helps to season the meat, bring out
its flavor, and keep it juicier once it's
cooked. I get mad if I don't have the time
or ability to let a piece of meat sit with
salt for a while before I cook it.

Mighty Maple

Serves 4

Pork has a bad reputation. My mom's generation roasted a lot of dry, bone-white big pork loins and called it the "other white meat." Pork shouldn't be bone white—that's often just bad, factory-farmed pork. And a pork loin is better off as a pork chop. But the loin's cousin, the tenderloin, is literally the filet mignon of pork. It's dark in color and smaller, a little meat log you can roll around, char on all sides, and cook quickly. It's the perfect weeknight piece of pork, with any side you like—sweet potato, salad, rice, whatever.

Tenderloin

2 1-pound	pork tenderloin
	kosher salt
	extra-virgin olive oil
5	shallots, quartered
1	Fresno chile
5	garlic cloves, crushed
1/4 cup	maple syrup
2 Tbsps.	salted butter
	Pepper Mix (page 285)
	parsley (optional)
	wilted greens (optional), for serving

Sprinkle the pork with salt a day or at least a few hours before cooking. Wrap it in plastic and refrigerate.

Coat the pork with a little oil and preheat a skillet over high heat. Add the pork and cook, turning and flipping it often, until it is well browned and about 150° F. Transfer the pork to a cutting board to rest.

Add the shallots to the skillet and let the cut sides color a bit before adding the chile and garlic. Let them cook for around 10 minutes before adding the maple syrup and butter.

Slice the pork and place the medium-cooked meat back in the skillet. Spoon and toss the sauce all over the pork before serving. Season with salt and pepper and garnish with some parsley and/or wilted greens. (The greens can be wilted down in the skillet after you remove the finished pork.)

Fermented Maple - Chile

Workday Quencher "Switchel"

Makes about 1 cup

Traditionally, switchel is not a fermented beverage—it's a mix of cider vinegar and maple syrup, spiced up with other things and diluted with water. It's nature's Gatorade, a great electrolyte-refilling, very refreshing beverage. It's also the perfect drink to start the day with. Drink an ice cold cup of this in the morning and put on your seat belt, your day is getting going.

I fell in love with switchel in bottled form. So why not take what I love about my favorite switchels—maple, ginger, chile, garlic—and ferment it? It can't not make it better. Better flavor. More depth. Probiotics. Amino acids. This recipe makes a concentrated base that's easy to dilute. You'll find the ratio that works for you. It's amazing in a cocktail, too.

1 cup	dark maple syrup
2	fresh cayenne chiles, crushed
150 grams	grated ginger
1/2 tsp.	salt
	lemon juice, for serving
	mint sprigs and lemon slices, for garnish

Place the maple syrup, chiles, ginger, and salt in a clean pint jar; or seal them securely in a vacuum bag (see Notes on Fermentation, on next page). If using a jar, use a rubber band to secure cheesecloth over the mouth, or seal it with a lid.

Let the jar or bag sit at room temperature for 3 to 5 days to ferment. You will see it active with bubbles—watch it. When you take a sniff, it should smell pretty good. Gingery, syrupy—not bad funky, good funky. And not too funky.

If using a jar, once a day, remove the cloth or unscrew the lid and stir, trying to leave the solids submerged under the syrup; they have a tendency to float. A sealed jar will need to be "burped" every day or so to release gas even if you do not stir it.

If using a vacuum bag, you do not need to agitate the ingredients daily. The bag keeps the ingredients in contact with one another and does not need to be stirred.

After 3 to 5 days, strain the liquid and discard the solids. Store the liquid in the fridge for a few days.

To make a drink, pour an ounce or so of the syrup into a glass of ice water. Add lemon juice to taste and stir well. Garnish with a little mint and lemon.

Notes on Fermentation

A few tips to help make your ferments turn out successfully.

Ingredients

Rinse them to remove any visible dirt and cut out blemishes or rotten spots. They can taint or otherwise screw up the final product. Use organic ingredients, the best you can find.

Equipment

Clean your equipment thoroughly. Thoroughly sanitize the utensils and containers you will use—including your hands—and any weights needed to keep the solids you're fermenting submerged under brine. I prefer glass or glazed ceramic weights, but you just want something reusable, easy to clean, and nonporous, so it doesn't give off or take in flavors.

Smell

This is a great indicator for whether the fermentation has gone off the rails. Does it smell bad? Not just *funky,* when you first open a ferment, but really bad. Open it, let it breathe for a sec, then sniff. It should smell like a slightly decomposing version of the original ingredients. If it smells like hot garbage, get rid of it. And if you try it and it tastes bad or rotten, toss it.

Bad growth

Vibrant colors like reds, pinks, funky yellows, and black are signs that you definitely want to pull it and start over: The types of bacteria, molds, or funguses that produce these colors are dangerous. But whites, blues, and greens—the colors you see on cheese or bread left in the cabinet for too long—are fine. Just scrape it off. Of course, if that freaks you out, go ahead and start over.

Get a kitchen scale

Your cup or tablespoon may be a little different than mine, but a gram is a gram no matter whose kitchen you're in, so you can be exact. That's particularly important when you're starting off and not yet comfortable eyeballing a measurement. Take the time to be careful. If you're going to do all the work for a fermentation project, you don't want to screw it up. You already bought the ingredients and put in the time to babysit the fermentation—the last thing you want is to throw it in the garbage.

Many recipes use 1.5 to 2 percent salt by weight as a rule of thumb to inhibit the development of harmful bacteria while lacto-fermenting vegetables (which itself creates an acidic environment hostile to those same harmful bacteria). When such a percentage is called for, it means you must weigh the ingredients you wish to ferment and multiply that number by the percentage to obtain the amount of salt to include in the brine you are making. For example, if the ingredients weigh 750 grams and the recipe calls for 2 percent salt by weight, you need 15 grams of salt. If you use more salt, the dish may become so salty it's inedible. If you use too little, it may taste underseasoned and, more importantly, there could be conditions in which the wrong bacteria could thrive. Salt is not the only factor inhibiting the growth of harmful bacteria, but it is an important one.

Jars should be covered

with cheesecloth secured around the mouth with a rubber band, just to keep the bugs out. You can also screw on a lid. If you do use a lid, make sure to "burp" the fermentation regularly (open the lid to let gas escape) so pressure does not build up inside the jar. You can purchase "airlock" fermentation lids with valves that allow gas out, but not in, and so do not require burping.

I sometimes use vacuum-sealed bags

for ferments like this one for the switchel concentrate, which doesn't produce a lot of gas. Vac bags keep the contents in contact with one another and help keep colors bright. You wouldn't want to use a bag for more active fermentations, like kimchi or sauerkraut, because you'll be building up lots of gas and don't want a blowout.

Vac bags are great because you can release the gas once the fermentation is complete, then re-seal the bag and store it in the fridge as a self-contained little packet.

I cut the bags long and wash them out and re-use them. I have one I cut long and only ferment chiles in it; I might get three or four batches of hot sauce or sambal out of a single bag. The plastic does get stained and picks up odor from what it holds, so I wouldn't re-use that bag for something like fruit.

The kind of vacuum sealer I use is a FoodSaver. There is a moist setting and a dry setting—I find neither one seals very well, so I usually leave some head space and seal the bag three times. I set the sealer on the edge of the counter and let the bag hang down, holding it with one hand. With the other, I hit the suction button. As it sucks, I watch the air go out. When you're bagging a liquid, it becomes a timing game. It happens fast, so I race to hit the seal button. It's fine if you don't get it perfect—the bag doesn't have to be as tight as a fish's ass. But I do get really excited when I get a solid wet seal.

Err on the side of caution.

When in doubt, throw it away and start over. If you want to experiment, do some research and give it a shot. For more information on the science and history of fermentation, as well as additional information on safety, making your ferments successful, and ideas for new projects, *The Art of Fermentation* by Sandor Ellix Katz and *The Noma Guide to Fermentation* by René Redzepi and David Zilber are excellent resources.

Fermented Garlic Maple Syrup

Makes about 2 cups

This is a riff on one of my favorite things to ferment, garlic honey. The same technique works well with maple syrup. If you've made my garlic honey before, you know that it starts out thick but gets thinner over time. Starting with syrup, the result becomes thinner still. I use it as a garlicky, sweet, umami enhancer in salad dressings, marinades, braises, and soups.

Don't be alarmed if the garlic cloves turn blue in the first week or two. This is a very common occurrence. Over time this blueness will fade and the garlic cloves will become translucent amber nuggets—and yes, you can eat them, too.

2 cups   maple syrup
20   garlic cloves (about 2 heads), medical grade, crushed

Combine the maple syrup and garlic in a quart jar and stir to combine, making sure all the garlic is coated in syrup. Use a rubber band to secure cheesecloth over the jar's mouth, or seal it with a lid.

Let the jar sit at room temperature for at least one week. Every day or so, remove the cloth or unscrew the lid and stir. A sealed jar will need to be "burped" every day or so to release gas even if you do not stir it.

Store the sealed jar in the fridge and use the syrup in any cooking application that could benefit from a savory-sweet garlic-maple flavor.

When I say "medical-grade" garlic I mean the best you can get—grown locally and so flavorful it burns your mouth when you eat it, not the dry and bland stuff. I joke around about it but great garlic is as much medicine as it is food! Like anything else in this book, it's a home run when you can get good ingredients from a reliable, traceable source. "You get what you pay for" is usually true.

Cup O' Belly

My friend Sue Li, a food stylist, used to make a version of her mom's three-cup chicken for family meal. That dish is a standard in Chinese and Taiwanese cooking, and its name comes from the use of soy sauce, rice wine, and sesame oil in the basic recipe, though the variations are almost endless.

This recipe for glazed pork belly begins with my memory of those flavors, though it's pretty far afield from the inspiration of Sue's mom's chicken. I've added more than a few Brad-isms and flavor riffs along the way. It's now an adaptation that I've grown into cooking often for my family. Thank you, Sue.

3 pounds	pork belly
1 cup	white wine
1/2 cup	soy sauce (I used shoyu)
1/4 cup	mirin
1/4 cup	maple syrup
6	garlic cloves
3	scallions, cut into ½-inch pieces
2 tsps.	grated fresh ginger
1 piece	dried kombu (kelp)
1	chile de arbol
1/2 stalk	lemongrass, thinly sliced
10	shiitake mushrooms, stems removed, caps sliced (optional)
2 cups	water

Preheat the oven to 325° F. In a heavy Dutch oven or roasting pot, sear all sides of the pork belly over medium-high heat.

Add the remaining ingredients to the pan. Bring to a simmer. Cover the pan and place in the oven. Braise for 2 ½ hours. Uncover the pan and continue to cook until the pork is fork-tender, about 30 minutes or so; removing the lid will allow the sauce to reduce a bit and also let the exposed pork caramelize.

Remove the pork from the sauce. Slice the pork and spoon some of the sauce over it. I love to serve this hot over rice or noodles, but it can be eaten with just about anything!

Glazed Baby

Turnips

Serves 4

Baby white turnips are a treat from nature. If you think you don't like turnips, get your hands on some Hakureis, and they'll change your mind. They eat more like a creamy radish than the well-known big brother turnip that most people know (or think they know).

Some folks love to hate on turnips and rutabagas, but they're fantastic. Let's make turnips and rutabaga cool. This recipe for them is easy and, surprisingly, satisfies my children.

3 Tbsps.	olive oil
2 Tbsps.	salted butter
3 bunches	baby white turnips, (such as Hakurei), quartered (leave the greens on but pick off any yellow or bad ones)
1	shallot, minced
1/2 cup	maple syrup
3	garlic cloves, grated
1 tsp.	grated ginger
2 Tbsps.	rice vinegar
	kosher salt
	pink pepper

Over medium high heat, heat the oil and butter in a large skillet until the butter is melted and mixed in with the oil. Add the turnips. (I cook these turnips with the greens on; just pick off any yellow or bad leaves.) Sear the cut sides for a few minutes before adding the remaining ingredients. Flip the turnips around often and watch to make sure the garlic doesn't burn.

These turnips don't need to be cooked until mushy; I cook them as I would radishes—just until they're tender. Adding a little fermented ramp miso (page 64) won't hurt this dish either, if you're feeling up to it!

Maple

Oatmeal

Makes about 4 servings

Oatmeal is a chance to play around and use whatever flavor combinations you want for your toppings. What's nice about this version is blooming the flavors of the nuts and other ingredients in butter before adding them to the oats. I chose mulberries, pistachios, cocoa nibs, and so on, but you can't go wrong with any dried fruit or nut or classic granola-y topping. Whatever your favorite dried trail mix fixin's are, go for it.

3 1/2 cups	maple sap or water
1/8 tsp.	salt
2 cups	rolled oats
3 Tbsps.	salted butter
1/4 cup	pistachios
1/4 cup	cocoa nibs
1/4 cup	dried mulberries
1/4 cup	goji berries
1/3 cup	coconut chips
3 Tbsps.	maple syrup
1	banana, sliced
1/2 cup	blueberries

Bring the sap or water and salt to a boil in a medium saucepan. Stir in the oats. Turn the heat to medium-low. Cover and cook for about 5 minutes, or until the oats are cooked to your liking. Add more sap or water if you want looser oats.

Meanwhile, in a small saucepan or skillet, melt the butter over medium-low heat. Add the pistachios, cocoa nibs, mulberries, goji berries, coconut, and maple syrup and let them "bloom" in the butter; the butter will foam, and that's okay. Stir often and let cook for a couple minutes.

Spoon some of the cooked oatmeal into a bowl and layer some banana and blueberries over top. Spoon some of the bloomed maple butter on top.

Catskill Mountains, New York, Early Spring

2

Home of the Ramps

My family has always respected and loved the woods. Not many people realize that 42 percent of New Jersey is covered by forest. Where I grew up, I was lucky to have direct access. In those woods I learned many things, both with my dad and with my friends. We kids foraged for wild raspberries, made forts, played in streams, climbed, got poison ivy, and learned about animals, plants, and nature every day. Total immersion in nature…It was a great way to grow up!

A massive patch

I have a keen memory of being in one particular place in the woods where there was a distinct smell. A good smell: peppery, mustardy, a little garlicky. It wasn't until later in life that I realized I was surrounded by ramps! Some people call them wild leeks or wild garlic. Ramps, like garlic, are in the allium family and are indigenous to forests in the Northeast. If you are ever walking through a lush green meadow or partially shaded forest in the springtime, you might smell that mustardy, peppery smell. If you do, tread lightly!

This chapter focuses on foraging and finding ramps locally. They truly are a treasure of the forest, often overlooked.

If you know me, you know I'm a big fan of foraging for food. Please know, however, that we have a great responsibility to protect and respect whatever we are foraging. I take this responsibility seriously. People like you and me, folks who love the outdoors, are shepherds of the land and the main line of defense in protecting it. Help me and please act responsibly, so my kids will have the opportunity to enjoy what Mother Nature provides.

Sadly, ramps have been overforaged for a long time, and they are now protected or regulated in some areas. If you are interested in foraging for ramps, check the local regulations in this regard.

The appearance of ramps means the end of winter and the birth of spring. They pop up in early March and are one of the first refreshing glimpses of new life in the forest that has been tucked in with snow all winter. As the snow melts, it leaves a wet, brown forest floor, creating the perfect conditions for growing. Ramps generally grow in clusters, often referred to as patches, and you see them erupting in these bunches from the snow or colorless landscape. Small bright shoots of green are a refreshing and welcome sight after the long cold months.

Look for tender, broad, bright green leaves, and stems with hues of white, pink, and red that shoot down the leaf to the bulb below. The bulb itself (which you'll see if picked correctly—that is, gently from the base) is bright white and can be as large as a thumb. The entire plant is edible and utilizing each part is essential. If you make the right friends or have access to land where you can manage to harvest some ramps, you're a lucky person.

This spring I was lucky. A friend of mine who grew up in the Catskills region of New York brought me to a ramp patch he's been managing and harvesting for years. Like most wild ingredients, the ramp is at the mercy of the weather and seasonal changes. Jason called me and said, "The mountain is looking good and the weather is lining up. You boys should head on up and we'll go pick some ramps in the morning"—or something like that.

I went online and quickly booked us a last-minute rental house in the middle of nowhere. Take my advice: Look at the details when renting a place, because photos can be deceptive. Granted, I don't need a fancy hotel everywhere I go, but this place didn't have running water or a toilet. It did have a wood-burning stove, though, so we made the best of it the first night and got drunk on

Whole ramps. I only take bulbs from
massive patches on private land.
If you're in doubt, only snip one of
the leaves above the bulb, and leave
the rest in the ground.

nice wine while sitting around a fire cooking sausages and talking politics. Situations like that are what you make of them, my friends. That's a little life lesson, folks…free with this book.

In the morning we woke up before the sun and Jason met us at our lovely place. He was impressed that we actually stayed the night, but the location was perfect and only a few minutes from the patch. Location, location, location! We threw some logs on the fire, grabbed our coffee, and headed over to a big barn to meet the guy who owns the land. We chatted and promised never to come back without Jason and to keep the location secret. He was a hell of a guy, and there's no way you're getting the name of the place from me.

We walked off a dirt road through a steep mountain pass. I started to see a few small ramp patches and think "Great, Jason got us here! Let's set up for a few pictures and get cooking." But as I paused, Jay chuckled and said we weren't there yet. Soon, we found ourselves in the largest ramp patch I'd ever seen—sunlit and green, a little slice of heaven. There were acres of a mountainside covered in gorgeous, deep-green ramps. I think I cried quietly to myself a little bit.

My friend and photographer Pat and I exchanged a look of amazement. The ramps were so thick that we had to tiptoe to walk without damaging them. Quickly we found a beautiful spot—every spot was beautiful—to set up a small fire and cooked lamb, ramps, and flatbread. (I'd carried this stuff on my back along with a few cast-iron pans and firewood.) We sat and ate with Jay, surrounded by the scent of ramps and the lush greens in the middle of the mountains. What a day. We took a bag full of ramps back home to make some favorite recipes. Please remember though, we picked a small amount from a private spot that is highly sustainable. Take care if you go foraging on your own, and do not destroy the population of an already vulnerable wild plant.

When it comes to cooking, there are obvious and easy uses for ramps: sautéed with scrambled eggs, on steak with butter, or in a burger. After all, ramps are great on anything that can use an oniony/garlicky pop. But since the season for ramps is so very short, I like to preserve them to enjoy throughout the year. Try fermenting them—a great way to bring them beyond their small harvest window in spring. Get creative!

Fermented

Spicy Ramps

Makes 1 quart

Ramps are eager to ferment and create a very active fermentation. Inspired by the hundreds of varieties of Korean kimchi made with different seasonings and vegetables, this recipe combines ramps with chile flakes, garlic, ginger, apple, and more to stretch the season for these special alliums. Once you have this in your fridge, you will put it on everything. Eggs. Pork chops. Pasta. Fish.

If you can't get ramps, you can substitute a 50/50 mix of scallion bulbs and garlic. Ramps have a big, spicy, fresh-garlic flavor to them that is totally unique, so it won't taste quite the same. But it'll still be good.

While you're making this, go ahead and use the leaves and tender stems to make the fermented salad recipe that follows.

2 pounds (907 grams)	ramp bulbs and red stems
20 grams	red pepper flakes, seedless
9 grams	kosher salt
1	green apple, cut into matchsticks
50 grams	ramp leaves, roughly chopped or left whole
1	garlic clove, peeled
10 grams	fresh ginger, grated
2 plugs*	mirin
4 plugs	fish sauce
100 ml (100 grams)	filtered water

In a large bowl, mix all of the ingredients together real nice and thoroughly.

Pack the mixture into your fermentation vessel of choice and weight the solids down with a glass or nonporous ceramic weight to keep them submerged in the brine. Cover with cheesecloth and secure it with a rubber band. Alternatively, use a container with an airlock to let gas escape. This fermentation is an active one, and it will get very bubbly and stinky (good things, in my book—see Notes on Fermentation, page 42).

Let the mixture ferment at room temperature for 3 to 7 days. The time will depend on your preference for how fresh and crunchy you want it. I like the ramps with a little crunch, so I often pull this on the younger side. If you ferment this for much longer at room temp, it will get stinky and the ramps will soften and become even more fragrant. More brine will form as the ramps ferment, so keep an eye on it and keep pushing the weight down when necessary, to keep the solids submerged.

Cap the container and put in the fridge where it will continue to ferment, more slowly, over the coming days and weeks.

What's a "plug"? I'm sorry, it's my brain's fault. Call it a Brad measurement—it's about a tablespoon. In twenty years the term ought to be universal.

Years ago, my friend and I were up in the Boundary Waters of Minnesota, the wilderness extending along the border between the U.S. and Canada west of Lake Superior. It's 1,500 miles of lake systems, where you portage your canoe from lake to lake, filter your own water, and, in our case, see only one other person for several days. We were completely detached: no phones, no nothing. French fur traders once used these lakes as a transportation system. Instead of horses, they relied on voyageurs paddling canoes.

It was one of the best trips of my life, the highest I've ever gotten, and there were definitely no drugs. We did, however, bring along a couple magnums of nice French wine, carrying it with us like we needed it to survive. As we rowed, we passed the magnum back and forth, giving each other a "plug" of wine. Thinking about it now, I guess we meant to say "glug." But I kept it, and now it's official.

Fermented Ramp

and Cucumber

Pickle Salad

Makes 1 quart

So you've gone and picked a big basket of ramps, and used the red stems for the previous recipe. Now you've got those tender stems and leaves. Sure, you can make a pesto with them. But one of my favorite ways to use them is in this pickled salad.

I'm not sure what to name it, but it sure is delicious. It's like a rampy cucumber-pickled giardiniera (ideal for an Italian sub). The herbs and sesame in the za'atar bring it to the Mediterranean. The bay leaves contribute tannins, which keep the cucumbers on the crunchy side even in a full-on sour fermentation.

Turn it into a spoon sauce by chopping it up and adding some olive oil, and put on a burger, a steak, or some fish. Or serve it simply as a fermented side salad.

2 pounds (907 grams)	ramp leaves and stems
2 pounds (907 grams)	cucumbers,
	cut into irregular bite-size chunks
27 grams	kosher salt
1 Tbsp.	Brad's Za'atar (page 227)
	or store-bought
1 Tbsp.	serrano chiles, sliced thin
8	bay leaves

So you just follow the same process as the Fermented Spicy Ramps (page 60), baby!

In a large bowl, mix all of the ingredients together real nice and thoroughly.

Pack the mixture into your fermentation vessel of choice, and weight the solids down with a glass or glazed ceramic weight to keep them submerged in the brine. Cover with cheesecloth and secure it with a rubber band. Alternatively, use a container with an airlock to let gas escape.

Let the mixture ferment at room temperature for 3 to 7 days. More brine will form as it ferments, so keep an eye on it and keep pushing the weight down when necessary, to keep the solids submerged.

Cap the container and put in the fridge where it will continue to ferment, more slowly, over the coming days.

Miso Ramp Bulbs

Makes about a pint

Miso-zuki is the Japanese technique of fermenting and preserving vegetables in miso. I've eaten ramp bulbs preserved this way at two years old. We pack ramp bulbs in miso and a bit of shoyu, let it sit at room temperature, and allow the bacteria and yeasts and enzymes and life forces in the miso to start working. The ramp bulbs leach a little liquid that mixes with the shoyu and then turn amber and translucent; meanwhile, the miso locks them in there and takes on the flavor of the ramps. It's a great preservation method, resulting in unique bulbs to slice and eat or use as garnishes, along with the infused miso to use in all your favorite miso applications. Two for one, baby!

250 grams	white miso
5 to 10 grams	shoyu (or your preferred soy sauce)
100 grams	ramp bulbs

In a small fermentation vessel of your choice, mix together the miso and soy sauce to make a slightly loosened paste. It will not be much looser than the miso on its own. Then pack in the ramp bulbs, making sure they're completely covered, like dinosaur eggs or fossils stuck in the mud.

Cover with cheesecloth secured with a rubber band, or with a lid. Let ferment at room temperature for one week. If using a lidded jar, release the gas every day or two.

I like to do this in a glass jar because the visual indicators of the process are so extraordinary. The miso-soy sauce mixture is a dense paste, and we've packed this moisture-filled organic material (the ramp bulbs) into it. As it starts to ferment, you'll start to see pockets of shoyu and ramp liquid start to form. The bulbs sit in their own liquids inside the little cavities, carving out their own spaces like an ant farm. As the bulbs release gas, the miso becomes aerated like a flaky biscuit, almost whipped. It's what I imagine fracking is like. The volume will increase by a third to a half.

Store the miso in a sealed container in the fridge, almost indefinitely.

Ramp Yogurt

Makes about 2 cups

I make lots of what I call spoon sauces: an oily/fatty, acidic combination that hosts a mixture of herbs, shallots, garlic, dried nuts, fruit, honey—layers that make it more delicious. Any spoon sauce is an open canvas that allows you to pick the direction you want to go, depending on what you're eating. Many cultures have a version of a spoon sauce; think chimichurri and salsa verde.

But I don't typically start a dish by thinking of the spoon sauce. I get excited about the vegetable or protein. That amazing spinach or chard, that piece of lamb or pork chop. Then I think about what would go well with it. This spoon sauce is fantastic with a dish with a little char on it, from flatbread to eggplant to grilled chicken thighs, or anything that wants a creamy sauce as a companion.

Spoon Sauce

2 cups	full-fat yogurt
3	ramps, whole
1	lemon, halved
1/4 cup	extra-virgin olive oil, plus extra to coat the ramps
	kosher salt, to taste
	Pepper Mix (page 285), to taste
3 sprigs	thyme, leaves only
1/2 tsp.	ground sumac

Heat a grill or grill pan to medium high. Scoop the yogurt into a medium bowl.

Coat the ramps and lemon halves with a little oil. Grill the ramps until soft and taking on a little color. Meanwhile, sear the cut face of the lemons on the grill to get a little caramelization on the fruit. Remove everything and let cool, then mince the ramps.

Add almost all of the ramps to the bowl with the yogurt. (I like to reserve some of the ramps, as well as the oil and seasonings, for a garnish.)

Squeeze the lemon juice in as well, and pour in half the olive oil. Stir well and taste, seasoning with salt and pepper mix and adding most of the thyme leaves and sumac. Stir again and adjust the acid and salt. Hell, adjust everything!

Garnish with the reserved grilled ramps (minced), thyme, and sumac. Drizzle the remaining oil on top.

Cast-Iron Ramp

Serves 4

These cast iron–seared lamb chops and ramps are a perfect springtime meal, especially if you get lucky with the weather and the mushroom gods and can find some morels to sear up. That's the home run I always hope for, but we didn't get one this year because of a late cold snap and some funky weather that kept the morels down. That's just the way it goes.

I love to serve the lamb and ramps with grilled sourdough flatbread. For each one, shape a fist-size ball (about 250 grams) of Brad's Sourdough (page 153) by hand into a 10- to 12-inch round with a little flour, then rub the round lightly with a little olive oil and/or lamb fat, salt, and your favorite spices. Cook in the skillet or over the fire, flipping often, until lightly browned and cooked through!

and Lamb

8	lamb loin chops
	kosher salt
1 to 15	morel mushrooms, dried or fresh (optional)
1/4 cup	dashi, wine, or water (if using dried morels)
8	ramps, whole
1/4 cup	extra-virgin olive oil
3 Tbsps.	salted butter
1	plug (see Note, page 61) vinegar or white wine
	Pepper Mix (page 285)

The day before you plan to cook the lamb, salt the chops and put in a bag in the fridge.

If using dried morels, soak them in a bowl of dashi, wine, or water for about 30 minutes, until soft and tender. Drain and pat dry.

Meanwhile, over a nice wooden fire in the forest or your grill back home, preheat a large cast-iron skillet to a good medium high.

Continues on next page

Continued
from previous
page

Coat the lamb and the ramps with the olive oil.
I like to first grill them together over the open
fire on a wire rack to get a nice smoky cook
going. Or you can drop them straight into the
cast iron if you want. Sear all sides and get a
good salty crust going on the chops.

When the meat is just about where you want
it in terms of doneness (I like medium rare),
if you have morels, slice them, add to the hot
skillet, and sear. Arrange the meat in the skillet,
bone side down, and add the ramps if you
seared them on the grate. Then add the butter
and let it melt. Cook, spooning that rampy
butter over the meat, for a minute or so. Just
before you pull the pan from the heat, hit it
with the plug of vinegar or wine, hit it with the
Pepper Mix, and let it reduce slightly. Slice the
lamb chops and eat them with your hands, or a
fork, along with the morels and ramps.

Long Island Sound, Late Spring

Eat More Squid

3

I am a big supporter of eating responsibly, accessing local resources, and respecting the animals that provide us sustenance while doing our best to maintain sustainability. From the onset of this book, I was determined to include a chapter about squid because it's a Northeast mainstay and an important member of the local food chain. But it often is overlooked. I personally think squid are a perfect food, rich in nutrients and abundant in number. These recipes encourage you to fish for it, prep it, and eat it responsibly!

I grew up with squid. My family and everyone else we knew ate it as fried calamari. It's typical Italian American fare, generally prepared in the same way: breaded, fried, and served with marinara sauce for dipping. Crispy batter on the outside with tender, sweet, white meat inside. What's not to appreciate? Kids loved it— who wanted the rings and who wanted the "spiders"? My dad used to bite the spiders with his teeth and wiggle the tentacles to get the kids to laugh (only to get chastised by my mom…or *his* mom).

Calamari freezes well and has meat that's palatable even to folks who aren't keen on seafood generally. Good squid doesn't eat like the "fish" most people identify with seafood; it's not flaky or a fillet, it's not a crustacean. (And don't call it a fish—it's a cephalopod.) I believe there is depth in flavor to squid, and variety in its preparation, that separates it from other seafood.

Squid are perfectly adapted to the world they live in. I joke that they look like they are from another planet because of their amazing adaptations and defense mechanisms. The evolutionary adjustments are noteworthy, from camouflage and changing colors to their methods of hunting and their great speed and agility. Their bird-like beaks and delicious (or terrible— depending on who you ask) tentacles explain how these creatures thrive so well in cold New England waters. Squid are one of my favorite creatures and one of my favorite ingredients to prepare. Rings, crazy eyes, big tubes, and purple tentacles make them look more like a creature from a sci-fi movie than what's for dinner tonight—but that's just part of their appeal! A squid would eat *you* if it could, that's for damn sure.

Squid species are found all over the world, but the New England ones are special to me. Squid season is in the late spring here, marked by huge schools or groups of squid coming in from the outer ocean to feed and spawn inshore. The big commercial fishing boats can't get that close to shore (three miles is the rule, I believe), which leaves the squid somewhat protected, vulnerable only to rod-and-reel anglers like myself.

Squid attack smaller fish or sea life with tentacles that splay out quickly to grab

their prey. Before the victim knows what's happening, the squid's beak-like mouth bites and shreds. If you were a small fish in the ocean, a 14-inch squid is what your nightmares would be made of.

My most recent squid-fishing experience began on a damp and rainy June afternoon in the mouth of Long Island Sound, near

the border of Rhode Island and Connecticut. I call this the T&T (tubes and tentacles) capital. Rhode Island has a fishing industry where many commercial boats and serious fishing outfits have set up shop. If you look at the frozen rectangular block of squid you see at your local supermarket, it will probably say "Caught in Rhode Island," and most of

the quality squid you eat at restaurants also come from these waters. Much respect to the hardworking Rhode Island fishermen!

You fish for squid at night, and this night was a tough one. Things started off calm but as the sun went down and our buckets of fresh-caught squid filled up, dense clouds descended on the water. In terms of

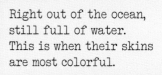

Right out of the ocean, still full of water. This is when their skins are most colorful.

successfully catching squid, we kicked ass, but the sea was rough and the night was one of the foggiest I've ever seen.

We were on my buddy Vinny's boat, and God bless his talented heart, he got us around the rocky coastline using nothing but his instruments and intuition. I couldn't see 5 feet in front of my face, let alone in front of the boat. But Vinny navigated the fog with ease, dodging lobster and crab buoys, rocks, and other obstacles. If I had been out there alone, I'd have been so fucked. Plus, the ocean was a cozy 59°F, so swimming to shore would not have been an option. I'd like to believe I'd make it, but then what? Soaking wet in the middle of the night on a beach miles from the car, trying to knock on someone's door before hypothermia sets in? No thanks!

The saying goes that "the best boat is your buddy's boat"—and I agree, especially when your buddy knows his shit. Vinny did, and because of his experience, we were never in a terrible position. But as he navigated, the water became increasingly rough. Kenyon, our photo assistant, and I both got seasick and ended up chumming the water twice. Big thanks to my pals for capturing those moments with photos that I hope never become public.

I've spent lots of time on the ocean, but these rough waters were a solid reminder that at sea, humans are small and nature is unforgiving. It's easy to go out on a bay that starts out flat as a lake, drinking beer with some friends, but things can go bad quickly. It sucked at times, but we caught the squid, got a few pictures, and had a great time doing it.

A word of caution to the landlubbers out there: You won't stop feeling seasick until you get back on land. Try to stay busy fishing or doing anything at all to keep your mind off it. But especially, don't go lay down in the cabin.

Back to the squid! You fish for them using really light tackle—even a lightweight freshwater rod and reel. Normal saltwater tackle outfits would be overkill for even large squid. The jig we used was a neon-colored weight dressed up like a little baitfish. Instead of the normal J-shaped fishing hook that most people are familiar with, squid-

fishing hooks are equipped with dozens of little spikes, like a weird mini grappling hook of needles facing up. By the way, all the oversize squid we caught were kept and frozen, set to use another day as swordfish bait—boat rules that I respect and promote.

Assuming the weather treats you well, squidding can be action-packed, good clean fun. Close to shore and usually not dangerously foggy, it's an easy fishing trip to pull off. There isn't much of a big fight when you hook a squid, and it's a perfect activity to do with kids or the elders. My nephew caught a whole bucket of them last summer off the coast of Narragansett on a charter. Get a squid in a kid's hand—or anyone's hand—and they will have no choice but to be in awe.

Catching squid is the fun and easy part. Cleaning them is an art of its own, requiring skill and patience. Squid are invertebrates and don't have a stiff bone structure like fish and other animals. Most people start by peeling off that beautiful color-changing skin, which is thinner than paper. Removal of the skin is not required, but some folks don't like the texture when prepared. I prefer to leave it on, because I like the way it cooks, turning bright red against the white meat.

Skin or no skin, you then need to remove the organs and alien-like goodies that come out of the long cylindrical body. Prepare for an inky mess—do this in the sink or outside over a bucket. The first time I cleaned a whole squid, I pulled out a long piece of what seemed to be a clear, flexible piece of plastic, but is actually the invertebrate skeleton. I couldn't imagine it wasn't man-made. You have to hold one to really understand.

Cooking and dressing the squid that you catch is extraordinary. From watching its colors change in your hands while the freshly caught squid wraps its tentacles around your fingers, to investigating their unique bodies, it's an experience that brings us up close and intimate with the food we eat. My favorite part of this adventure was when we were back on land, standing around a fire and grilling our fresh catch. From ocean to table…that's what it's all about. Eat more squid!

Grilled Squid Skewers

Serves 4

Here's an easy way to cook squid that's different and delicious.

Marinade

1/2 cup	Fermented Pepper Paste (page 100)
1/4 cup	honey
1/4 cup	extra-virgin olive oil
2 Tbsps.	soy sauce (I used shoyu)

1 pound	squid, tubes and tentacles, rinsed
12	wooden skewers, soaked in water if you have time
	Brad's Furikake (page 192) or sesame seeds, for garnish
	Thai basil or other fresh herbs, torn, for garnish
	lime juice, for serving (optional)

Combine all the marinade ingredients in a medium bowl and mix thoroughly. Pour half of the marinade into a gallon-size zip-top bag or another medium bowl, add the squid, and coat thoroughly. Reserve the other half of the marinade to use as a brushing sauce during grilling. Let the squid marinate in the fridge for at least half an hour or up to a day.

Prepare a grill or your fire to medium-high heat. Thread all the squid parts onto the skewers. Place the skewers on the grill and grill for about 5 minutes, turning and brushing them frequently with the reserved marinade. This will build a nice sticky glaze. The squid meat will turn bright white when cooked through.

Finish the squid with a sprinkle of furikake or sesame seeds and torn fresh herbs. A squeeze of lime juice wouldn't be bad either!

Chilled Squid Salad

Serves 4

Poaching squid in butter gives you perfectly tender and flavorful meat. I made this salad on our squid-fishing trip and we really enjoyed it. It was inspired by the classic Italian American seafood or squid salad that I grew up seeing in refrigerated deli cases. If it was a place you knew and trusted, you'd get it—otherwise you might take a pass.

Poached Squid

2 sticks (1 cup)	salted butter
1/2 cup	water
1	fresh chile, crushed
1	garlic clove, crushed
1 tsp.	freshly ground black pepper
1 pound	squid, tubes and tentacles, rinsed

Salad

1 cup	cracked, pitted Castelvetrano olives
1 cup	thinly sliced celery with tops
1/2 cup	chopped fresh parsley
1/2 cup	extra-virgin olive oil
1/4 cup	red wine vinegar
2 tsps.	dried oregano
1 cup	toasted skin-on peanuts, roughly chopped
	kosher salt and freshly ground black pepper

For the poached squid, in a medium saucepan, heat the butter, water, chile, garlic, and pepper over medium heat until the liquid reaches about 150°F. Add the squid and poach for a minute or two, just until the squid meat turns white and firms up in texture but is still very tender. Drain the squid, discarding the butter. Refrigerate until chilled, about 1 hour.

For the salad, in a large bowl, combine the olives, celery, parsley, olive oil, vinegar, oregano, peanuts, and chilled squid. Toss and season with salt and pepper to taste. Serve immediately, or refrigerate for just a couple of days.

Squid Toast

Serves 4

To avoid a rubbery texture, squid is usually cooked hot and fast, or low and slow. I crave it both ways. This recipe represents low-and-slow perfection. Think of the sauce like a squid fra diavolo—spicy and tomatoey—with squid that's tender but not mushy, just super soft. Braised this way, it doesn't taste like the ocean, but rather acquires a richer, deeper flavor that goes so well with the tomato sauce. It's great on grits, pasta, or toast, as it's served here. And I don't care what the Italians say, go ahead and put some Parmesan on top. I do it all the time.

1	small shallot, minced
1/4 cup	extra-virgin olive oil
3	garlic cloves, crushed, peeled, and chopped
1	dried chile de arbol, sliced
3 Tbsps.	white miso
1/4 cup	white wine
1 (28-ounce)	can crushed tomatoes
2 pounds	squid, tubes and tentacles, rinsed, tubes sliced into rings
3 Tbsps.	salted butter, plus more for the bread
	toasted bread
	grated Parmesan, to taste
	freshly ground black pepper, to taste

In a medium saucepan, sweat the shallot in the oil over medium heat for a few minutes. Add the garlic, chile, miso, and wine and let simmer for about 2 minutes. Stir in the tomatoes and allow to simmer on low for about 15 minutes, just to let the tomatoes get juicy and break down a little.

Add the squid and butter to the sauce. Cook the squid, stirring often, until it is white throughout and perfectly tender, about 45 minutes.

Lightly butter some nice toasted bread of choice and spoon the squid and some sauce over each piece. Cover with grated Parmesan and pepper.

Squid
Pizza

1 ball (about 250 grams)	Brad's Sourdough (page 153)
1/2 cup	sliced squid tubes and tentacles, rinsed
10	very thin, round lemon slices
10	very thin, round yellow squash slices
2 Tbsps.	extra-virgin olive oil, plus more for drizzling
1 Tbsp.	chopped capers
1 to 8	garlic cloves, thinly sliced
	kosher salt and freshly ground black pepper
	grated Parmesan
	Fermented Chile Honey (recipe follows)
	fresh basil or parsley for garnish

Makes 1 nice 10- to 12-inch pizza

Squid on pizza with some caramelized lemon and hot honey…just try it, trust me. If your knife skills aren't those of a sushi chef, use a mandolin to get paper-thin slices of the lemon and squash. Just watch your fingertips!

Place a large skillet or baking stone in the oven and preheat the oven to as high as it will go for 20 minutes.

Shape the dough into a 10- to 12-inch round, or the size you desire. Toss the squid, lemon slices, squash, olive oil, capers, garlic (as much as you want), and salt and pepper to taste together in a medium bowl until well mixed.

Dress the dough with the topping and spread it out evenly across the dough so that every slice will have a little bit of everything. Grate some Parmesan over the top. Bake in the skillet or on the stone for about 5 minutes, until the dough is cooked through and you've got a little color on both the rim of the crust and the bottom of the pizza. Just keep an eye on it as all ovens are different and rotating the pie might be required.

Drizzle the pizza with the fermented hot honey and more olive oil. Sprinkle with herbs and more black pepper and Parmesan if you like.

Fermented Chile Honey

I love the floral depth and heat that the habaneros bring, but you can also use aji, Thai, or cayenne peppers...whatever chiles you can get or grow will work for this bad boy. No rules, just riff around, maybe even add some sesame seeds! And remember, as with the Fermented Garlic Maple Syrup (page 44), the garlic may turn blue and float—but that's okay.

1 pint (16 ounces)	local raw honey
5	habanero chiles, seeded and thinly sliced
1	Fresno chile, sliced
1	serrano chile, sliced
1 to 2	garlic cloves, thinly sliced (optional)

Makes about 1 pint

This stuff is the best and can be put on almost anything...pizza happens to work perfectly. Drizzle it on fried chicken, brush it on grilled fish, put it on your pancakes—I don't care. You'd be surprised at the things a little heat and sweet can go with. It might not even suck on breakfast cereal.

The recipe is about as easy as it gets. Make sure to wash and remove any rot spots or blemishes from the chiles. Fermenting food isn't always about extending the shelf life of stuff that's about to go bad; I like to ferment with ripe and juicy fruits and veggies. For this recipe use the best you can find.

Combine all the ingredients in a quart jar and stir so all the chiles and garlic are coated in honey. Cover the jar with a piece of cheesecloth and secure with a rubber band, or seal it with a lid.

Let the contents ferment at room temperature for at least a week or up to a month—that's your call. Every day or two, give the contents a stir, leaving the contents submerged in honey and making sure to burp the jar to release any gases if it is sealed. It will get bubbly and loose. Seal the jar and keep it in the refrigerator for up to a couple weeks.

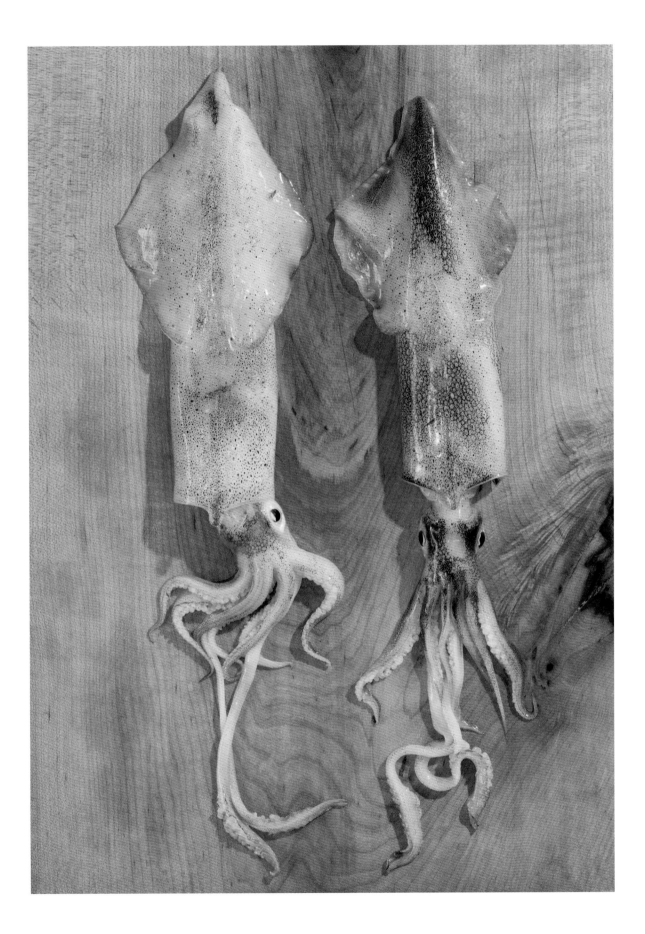

Pool Party

4

For folks who have never been to the New York City tri-state area in the middle of summer, the potential for disgusting amounts of humidity in the air, causing anything you are wearing to stick to you uncomfortably, is very real. On those days, no matter who you are you'll be looking for a place to relax by a pool or body of water. Growing up, I never had a pool. I still don't, for that matter. But I can't deny that I love to take a dip and cool off in one whenever I can. Swimming brings out the inner child in people, I've noticed, and I love that.

New York, Midsummer

Pools are like boats: The one your friend has is the best. Sorry, friends with pools, I love you. I promise I will never be dead weight when you invite me over. You can bet the farm I'll bring some top-notch homemade provisions. Hell, I'll even clean up, too.

But when the weather is that hot I never want to eat heavy food. Nobody wants to fire up the oven and braise lamb shanks on a 95°F day with 99 percent humidity. If you do know someone like that, it's a major red flag and I recommend being careful around them (I'm only sort of joking). That said, you still have to eat, and swimming around the pool, drinking refreshing cold beverages and seeing how many underwater laps you can do all day is known to work up some sort of appetite.

A great pool party spread is all about the things you can make ahead of time, and foods that can hang at room temperature. I've included a few recipes that I've been known to bring to a pool party or hot-day hang. I'm drawn to the grill and the ability to be outside while cooking. Sure, big fancy pools and grills and stonework are awesome, but what's great about cooking outside is that grills come in all sizes and shapes. You can have a huge outdoor built-in kitchen or a small portable grill that folds up.

Whether you are at a pool, a park, a backyard, or a beach, just remember summer barbecues don't need to just be hot dogs and hamburgers. Make a fermented pepper paste, like the one in this chapter inspired by sambal. It's great for anything on the grill and takes well to seafood or veggies, packing a nice punch and depth of flavor. Use it as a hot sauce or marinade. I always bring a jar with me.

Or take a chance with a familiar and crowd-pleasing dish like shrimp cocktail that can be made the day before. It is so easy to do at home and the difference in quality compared to the plastic rings from the supermarket filled with sad soggy shrimp is undeniable. Maybe grill some fruit and make a slightly salty and tangy fermented watermelon cocktail…go ahead, you earned it, babe!

Thoughtful food doesn't need to be super expensive. Just get the best ingredients you can and give it a go. Listen to your body and eat what makes you feel good. Soak it all in, play and eat around the pool with friends until you fall asleep like a little kid again. You need it. We all need to have more fun while cooking and eating.

A behind-the-scenes 35mm shot by
me, while Pat was in the pool

Grilled Fruits

Fermenting the fruit ahead of time is an option. Take five or six stone fruits of choice and/or some figs and cut them into big pieces. Weigh them, including the pits, and measure out 1 percent kosher salt and 1 percent sugar by weight. Combine the fruits, salt, and sugar in a bowl. You can add some cinnamon, cardamom, vanilla, or other spices or a chile for heat to the mix. Seal it all in a vacuum bag or half-gallon jar. Let the fruit ferment at room temperature for a week or so, until mushy, burping every day or so to release gas. Strain out the juice and save it for drizzling over a dessert (or use in a savory dish), then grill the fruit flesh as described above.

When you grill fruit you get that nice Maillard caramelization of its own sugars, plus a little smoky seared-ness. It's the same reason people like char marks on their steak: Crust is flavor. And it's fun. I grill a lot of plums and cherries—I love the way the skins blister up, and the insides can remain kind of cool, depending on how hot your fire is.

Along with being a great dessert, these grilled fruits are amazing with a steak or a pork chop. Just grill the fruit (hold the whipped cream), serve alongside steak, and you're there. Squeeze a lemon over it all before serving: The sour-sweet in-season natural flavors with beautiful medium-rare beef...it just elevates the whole meal.

These fruits can cook on a flat-top or griddle as well as a grill.

If you want to try fermenting the fruit before you grill it, see note opposite. Here's a little encouragement: Fermenting fruit is one of the oldest things that humans have done. That's how people started getting drunk originally. Fruit wants to ferment; it's sugar, carbohydrates, built-in fertilizer to re-create the tree it fell from. Controlling that fermentation and using it to develop flavors is one of the simplest things to do, but one of the trickiest things to do well. It's easy to make a simple sauerkraut but hard to make good wine.

1 cup	whipped cream
1/2 cup	mascarpone, whipped
1/4 tsp.	vanilla bean paste
	pinch kosher salt
	drizzle of maple syrup, plus more for serving (optional)
	oil or butter
4	mixed stone fruits, halved and pitted
10	fresh figs, halved if large, whole if small
20	whole cherries, pitted
1/2 cup	shelled pistachios, toasted and chopped
	fresh herbs for garnish

In a medium bowl, fold together the whipped cream, whipped mascarpone, vanilla bean paste, salt, and maple syrup. Keep cold.

Heat a grill, cast-iron skillet, or griddle to medium high. Brush the grate or surface with a little oil or butter. Brown the stone fruit, figs, and cherries, flipping and searing so all sides are cooked. Don't let the fruit get so soft it falls apart, but you want it to pick up nice caramelization. I cook the different types of fruit separately as they tend to cook at different rates, but you can cook them all at once if you're comfortable with that.

To serve, fill the bottom of serving bowls with the cream mixture and top with some fruit, maple syrup, and pistachios. A little mint, basil, or herb of choice won't hurt ya.

Charred Radishes

Serves 4

Radishes are one of my favorite foods—a gift from Mother Nature that needs no correction. Salt 'em, butter 'em, you know the classics. I eat them by the bushel. But I never thought of grilling them until recently. Just think: Tender, rooty things like radishes, all spice and snap, with their beautiful edible greens dressed in salt and olive oil—hell yes, grill 'em up! It becomes like a really beautiful warm salad of itself. Then put those grilled radishes over a yogurt spoon sauce like the one below (or in the ramp chapter, page 66) and you're in really good shape.

with Herby Yogurt

4 bunches	radishes with greens, left whole if small and halved if large
	extra-virgin olive oil
	kosher salt and black pepper
	full-fat Greek yogurt
1/2 cup	finely chopped mixed herbs
2 Tbsps.	lemon juice
	Pepper Mix (page 285), to taste
	shaved pecorino Toscano cheese, for garnish

Toss the radishes with some oil and salt and pepper and grill over high heat. (A cast-iron grill pan or skillet, or any way you'd cook a steak, will also work.) You want to sear the sides of the radishes hot and fast to get some tasty color on them without cooking them through so they get mushy…although I kinda like a few like that too.

Mix the yogurt, herbs, lemon juice, pepper mix, and a little more olive oil together in a medium bowl. Serve the radishes on top of the herby yogurt or serve it alongside as a dip. Top with shaved cheese. This dish is an open book, so play around and have at it!

Fermented Pepper Paste on left,
and Fermented Chile Hot Sauce
on right

Fermented

Makes about 1 quart

This is a great lacto-fermented briny hot sauce, perfect to make with local chiles, or ones you've grown yourself. (Get the best stuff you can find.) You can customize the recipe to include other chiles or spices you love and match the flavor profile to your cooking.

As much as I love this hot sauce, I also really enjoy its byproduct, which I call "table brine." It's a great base for other dishes. Almost a hot sauce on its own, it's a great jumpstart for other dishes: with smoked fish or brined or marinated meats, or as an addition to dressings or soups for a zinger.

You can also take this same recipe, cut out the water, and ferment it all in a jar or vac bag, then blend it with your choice of vinegar. That will stabilize the hot sauce, which will be much more acidic than the recipe below. Every time I want to make hot sauce I do it this way or that way, and I go back and forth.

Chile Hot Sauce

2 pounds	hot chiles of choice (Fresno, aji, and/or habanero)
6	garlic cloves, peeled
3	dried morita chiles
3	dried hibiscus flowers
	kosher salt, 2 percent by weight
2 quarts (8 cups)	water
1/4 cup	rice vinegar

Rinse the chiles thoroughly and cut out any mold or bad boo-boo spots and remove the stems. If you want the full power of the chiles' heat, leave in the seeds. Halve them if you like.

Weigh the trimmed fresh chiles along with the garlic, dried chiles, and hibiscus flowers, then measure out 2 percent of that weight in kosher salt.

Add the water, salt, and all the other ingredients except for the rice vinegar to a gallon-size jar

Continues on next page

Continued
from previous
page

with a cloth lid or airlock so it does not need to be burped regularly. Let ferment at room temperature for about 2 weeks, until its bubbles start to calm down. I have messed with shorter and longer ferments, and you should too.

Strain the liquid off and reserve it. I call this table brine, and it's fantastic to cook with or put in drinks. Remove the hibiscus flowers, which would change the color of the sauce.

Put the chiles and garlic into a blender and add the rice vinegar. Blend and add a little of the reserved table brine to get the consistency you like best.

You can keep the sauce at room temperature if you're eating it fast and often, but store it in the fridge to keep longer, up to a few weeks. If it's a young ferment, the sauce will continue to ferment in the jar it's stored in, especially at room temperature.

Sauce separation is natural. There are stabilizers like agar agar or xanthan gum that you can mess with if you want, but that's never been my thing. I just give the jar a good shake before I use it. Sometimes I blend a little oil in, but warning: That will change the color.

Fermented

Makes 1 to 2 pints

Here's a riff on the common practice of fermenting peppers with salt and spices to use as a base for cooking. Turned into a smooth sauce or chunky paste, it's a powerhouse of umami and heat. It's a great condiment to keep in the fridge to use often on seafood, veggies, meats, and more. While many cultures use chile pepper pastes in their cooking, this one's ingredients are inspired by Indonesian sambals. You can remove all or some of the seeds from the peppers if you want to dial back the heat.

Pepper Paste

1 pound	Fresno and cherry chile peppers, minced
4-inch piece	fresh ginger, grated
8	garlic cloves, peeled
2 Tbsps.	tamarind paste
	kosher salt, 1.5 percent by weight
	grated zest and juice of 1 lime
	couple dashes of fish sauce
	sesame seeds and sesame oil to fold in at the end of fermentation (optional)

Weigh the chile peppers, ginger, garlic, and tamarind paste, then measure out 1.5 percent of that weight in kosher salt. Combine the salt and all the other ingredients except for sesame seeds and sesame oil in a vacuum bag or quart jar. If using a jar, cover it with cheesecloth secured with a rubber band, or seal with a lid.

Allow to ferment at room temperature or in a warm place for at least a few days or up to a couple weeks, until its bubbles start to calm down. If using a jar with a lid, burp it to release gas every day or so. Temperature will determine fermentation speed here: In the summertime, your ferments will move along much more quickly than in the winter. Find a sweet spot… 80°F is pretty sweet.

Pour the mixture into a blender and pulse until it reaches your desired consistency. It can be left as chunky or smooth as you'd like. I like to mix sesame seeds and sesame oil into the mixture before I serve it or store it in the fridge, for up to a couple weeks.

Shrimp Cocktail

Serves 6

When it's done right, shrimp cocktail is the best, and it's been the best forever. It's a timeless classic that never went anywhere. The problem with shrimp cocktail's reputation comes from soggy, flavorless, poorly farmed shrimp that you get in a plastic ring at some semi-okay supermarket, where the best thing is the cocktail sauce masking how gross the shrimp really is.

Having access to really awesome shrimp changes things. Shrimp freeze well, so you can make this if you don't have a fresh source. All you need to do is take some small preparations as below, to make sure you get a snappy, poppy shrimp.

(Because I Love It So Much)

2 1/2 pounds	large shrimp
2 1/2 Tbsps.	kosher salt
1/2 tsp.	baking soda
3 quarts	water
3 cups	white wine
1	celery stalk
1 stalk	lemongrass, trimmed and crushed
2	shallots, peeled
	handful mixed herbs, leaves and stems
1 knob	fresh ginger
5	garlic cloves, crushed and peeled
1 tsp.	peppercorns
1 tsp.	Old Bay seasoning
5	bay leaves
	cocktail sauce (see Fermentation Bonus)

Peel and devein the shrimp, leaving the tail segments intact. Set the shells aside.

Toss the shrimp, 1½ teaspoons of the salt, and the baking soda together in a bowl and let sit for about 30 minutes in the fridge. This will help you get nice snappy, plump shrimp.

Combine the reserved shrimp shells, the remaining 2 tablespoons salt, and all the remaining ingredients except the cocktail sauce in a large pot. Bring everything to

Continues on next page

Continued
from previous
page

a gentle simmer and simmer for about 20 minutes. Strain out all the solids and return the stock to the pot. It will be used to poach the shrimp.

Place the pot over medium heat, but do *not* let the stock return to a boil. Use a thermometer to bring the stock to 175°F and no higher.

Meanwhile, prepare an ice bath and have several zip-top bags ready to rapidly cool down the shrimp after it is poached.

Once the poaching liquid has reached 175°F, add the shrimp. Over medium-low heat, allow the liquid temperature to get back to 165°F or 170°F maximum. Once it reaches that temperature, take the shrimp out. They should be opaque and tender.

This next part is a little annoying but worth it: Using a slotted spoon, scoop out the shrimp and place 12 or so at a time into each bag, then dip into ice water to shock and chill. Remove them when they're cold. This will help all that flavor we worked into the poaching liquid stay in the shrimp and not get sogged out in bland cold water. You'll have flavorful and snappy cold cocktail shrimp to serve with your favorite **cocktail sauce**. Do a day ahead if you want!

Fermentation Bonus: If you want to make a fermented cocktail sauce, you've got to start ahead of time. Add 0.5 percent kosher salt by weight to fresh grated horseradish and garlic and let ferment for a day or two. Then fold it into ketchup or Heinz chili sauce with a little lemon, or use it to jazz up your favorite cocktail-sauce base.

Fermented Watermelon

Drink

Serves 6

I don't think I know a single person who doesn't like watermelon. Nice and bright, it's a perfect fruit. Like the radish, a watermelon is perfect the way nature made it; there's nothing I could change. I like it ice cold and can eat tons of it fresh.

Of course, there is a lot of water in them—the name says it all. If it's been a watermelon season and there's a lot to go around, try sacrificing one to make this juice. It's very refreshing. I'm not a watermelon-gazpacho guy, but you can make a pretty great cocktail with this. It needs no more sweetness, but add some more herbs or some switchel (page 40), then freeze it to make ice pops that are great for the kids, and good for the grandma.

Continues on
next page

Continued
from previous
page

3 pounds	watermelon meat
1 tsp.	kosher salt
3 sprigs	fresh mint
2	fresh basil leaves
pinch	cayenne

Combine all the ingredients in a vacuum bag or large jar. If using a jar, cover it with cheesecloth secured with a rubber band, or seal with a lid.

Let the mixture ferment at room temperature for 2 to 3 days, until the flesh of the fruit breaks down and turns into thick red juice. Use your hands to help break up the chunks of fruit over the days. If using a sealed jar, make sure to burp it to release any gas every day or so.

Strain the mixture through a fine-mesh strainer and serve chilled over ice or with seltzer. I love to pour it over ice with a couple ounces of mezcal or tequila, a sprig of mint, and some lime juice. Use within a day or two.

I sneakily took a behind-the-scenes shot of the real food-styling pros taking a break here.

Callen and his crabs

Blue Claws, Baby

The blue crab's Latin name is *Callinectes sapidus*, which roughly translates as "beautiful savory swimmer." That could not be more on point! This particular species has gorgeous colors, from blueish green to even red, with shades in between. But as pretty and delicious as they are, blue claw crabs aren't everyone's favorite. I figure it's due to the amount of work required for a small amount of meat. But, don't let that turn you off: The effort is worth it!

5

The family sitting down and putting work in on the crabs. There's no other way I'd rather eat them.

Two buddies stoked on catching
the first monster blue claw

I think loving blue crabs is in my DNA. Come to think of it, I never had a chance not to love them, as crabbing has been a family activity since I was younger than my kids are now. It's like fishing but easier, a fun and inexpensive way to catch your own food. Some of the biggest crabs I've ever caught were on handlines with a fish head tied to the end. Hours of crabbing fun for under five bucks, folks! That's assuming you already have a net, but a total expenditure of $40 will set you up for the season. I know some local guys who just go around in kayaks at night and scoop crabs off the dock pilings. Everyone has their favorite spots off docks, piers, or little boats.

Catching the Buggers

My crabbing memories always took place "down the shore," as we Jersey natives refer to the state's entire beach region. We vacationed here every year of my childhood and crabbing was mandatory. My mom, dad, sister, and hell, I think even the dog came too, along with cousins and friends. My mom is a handline legend, the most gentle line-puller I've ever met. Big fat crabs don't even know they are coming up off the bottom when Mom gets on that line.

There are other ways to catch crabs, but handlines are the simplest (and hardest) way, and I love that. Not familiar? Just hit a local bait shop near the coast and ask for a handline and some bunker. The handline consists of a long (probably 25-foot) sturdy cotton cord and a small (1- to 2-ounce) clip weight. You add your bait to the end and drop it down into the deep water. Tie the line to the dock, a rail, or anything really, but check it often for movement or little tugs. That's the crab nibbling. If you think you have something, ever so slowly pull the line up, hand over hand. You have to be slow and gentle to avoid spooking the greedy bunker eater on the end. As you pull, you'll begin to see him a few feet down...get that net ready and SCOOP!

Don't be discouraged if they swim away. It happens to the best of us.

In addition to handlines, I use wire cage traps. My dad's traps are tried and true, and probably thirty years old. Basically, they're weighted wire boxes with doors on the sides that flap open when the cage hits the bay bottom. You tie the bait securely on the inside and throw the whole thing into the water. The perfect throw takes some skill, and it feels really good when you nail down your tossing technique. After the traps are thrown, you wait 10 to 15 minutes or so, depending on how action-packed the day has been. Don't get impatient and pull up too soon; you need to give the crabs a chance to find the bait and get inside. Unlike handlines, which take some skill and finesse to retrieve, you pull these traps up super hard and super fast. That quick action pulls the trap doors shut and keeps the monsters inside. Every pull is like Christmas—you never know what you are going to get.

Crabbing season starts in spring and extends into the fall, but summer is prime time because these back fin swimmers cover a lot of ground and move with the tides. There are some parameters as to size and what you can keep, so bring a ruler and be careful to follow local regulations. Generally, you have to measure point to point on the shell, and it's important to throw back the little ones. Even though blue claws are in abundance off the Jersey shore, we have to respect how we can sustain and care for the species.

After the crabs are caught, you've got to get them off the line or out of the trap and into a basket. This is not an easy task! After a few tries, you'll know where the term "crabby" comes from. These buggers are tenacious and have attitude. Every crabber has a little trick on how to handle; grab by the far back flipper, I say. But, however you do it, don't get pinched. After all these years, my sister still gets clamped down on every time. Recently she almost lost a nail and we heard about it all day. Be careful, but act quickly or they will scramble away.

Bait

"Bunker" is a slang term for menhaden, which I believe is one of the most important fish species in the Northeast. Huge schools cruise the beaches and everything wants to eat them, including our bottom-dwelling crab pals. I think this is the best type of bait for crabs; it's cheap, in abundance, and a natural, native food source.

You'll see a lot of people use chicken legs or chicken necks as bait. It certainly works well and doesn't fall apart like a fish will over time in the water. That being said, I don't use chicken and never have. No judgment here, but my reason is that chicken bones don't naturally fall to the ocean floor. Do the crabs care? No, not at all, I'm sure they love the treat. But I care. It just always seemed more responsible to me to use the abundant local food source, something in the crab's natural diet or environment.

It's certainly not the worst problem out there, I know that. It just sits wrong with me when I see the garbage can by the pier overflowing with chicken packaging. People leave the bones and scraps all over and it seems unnatural and careless to litter the place with bacteria that don't belong there. I encourage everyone who wants to get involved in the outdoors to do so, but please leave it cleaner than it was when you got there. Whenever I go crabbing, I end up picking up other people's trash.

Then and Now

I grew up crabbing with my family, but after high school I took a break. Life is funny that way; you go through ages and stages but come back to your true interests in the end. One thing I'm grateful for now is that by learning to crab with my family, I learned the ropes and some valuable skills so that later I had knowledge and could develop my own crabbing methods as an adult.

I got back into crabbing in my mid-twenties, about the time I had moved to Brooklyn and enrolled in culinary school. One day I was on a bike ride passing the lovely Newtown Creek Wastewater Treatment Plant in Brooklyn (Google it). I saw a van pulled over to the side, and a man throwing crab traps and handlines into the water.

My first thought was I wouldn't want to fall into that water, let alone eat from it. But there he was, struggling with a handline by himself. It is difficult to carefully bring up the line and scoop with the net at the same time. I dropped my bike and walked over. We didn't speak the same language, but we did speak fluent crab. He looked me in the eye and knew I was down to help. He handed me the net and I helped him nab one of the biggest male blue claw crabs I've ever seen. We're talking a 7-inch point-to-point monster, folks. I always looked for that crabber later, but never saw him again.

My interest in crabbing had been piqued,

Crabbing gear

Bonus Recipe Riff: I always keep a couple
extra crabs on hand to add to tomato
sauce. It's an incredible thing, and I do
it every year. Basically add some dried
chile flakes and garlic to the sauce
recipe (page 144) from the Tomato Love
chapter. Then throw in some whole crabs
and simmer them like they were meatballs
for a couple hours. Maybe simmer up some
sliced squid and clams as well, and you
got yourself one hell of a twist on a red
sauce, bud. Enjoy!

but the trouble was that most of my friends didn't want to wake up early and drive to sit on a dock, trying to catch crabs that aren't guaranteed to bite. And even when they do, it's work to get the meat! I get it. But, allow me to introduce my buddy, Adam. Before my move to the big city, I lived in a small farmhouse in rural New Jersey with a bunch of people, one of whom was Adam Papanestor. He and I both grew up in the same town, and though he's a couple years older than me, we've always had a special bond. My family calls him Uncle Doom (my kids too), which isn't a description of his attitude, it's just because he listens to a lot of Doom Stoner Metal. If you aren't familiar with the genre, look it up.

Anyway, Adam and I both surfed a little out on Long Island. While out there, I kept noticing little spots that looked super crabby. I thought if there was that guy catching monsters in a questionable creek in Brooklyn, there must be some good crabs out in the

beautiful Long Island Sound. I sure as hell wasn't wrong. So, since Adam is always up for something, he turned out to be my #1 crabbing buddy.

We started to crab out there pretty regularly, and through the years one thing we noticed was the diversity of the people we encountered. Our fellow crabbers were always in larger groups, whole families really, out enjoying the day and crabbing together. It was beautiful…from a grandma to little kids barely old enough to pull a line up. It warmed my heart to see so many families passing down this tradition that was such a part of my childhood.

Every time we're out there, we make new acquaintances and pull up all types of little creatures from the water: green spider crabs, blowfish that puff up when you handle them, snails, and seaweeds. It's like a little biology class. Till the day I die, I will always be that little kid checking lines and traps for an educational or tasty treat!

Family

Steamed Crabs

Makes 1 dozen crabs

Old Bay steamed crabs! These crabs are best cooked in a large lobster steamer pot, which I'm sure you all have by now...and if you don't, you need to get one ASAP. They're great pots for all types of big cookout activities, but really fantastic for steaming whole live crabs. I use an outdoor propane burner like the ones people use at Thanksgiving to deep-fry turkeys (and burn sheds down with). Like the steamer pot, an outdoor propane burner is another must-have unit if you have the outdoor option. All of this can be done inside, and I've done it like that myself. All that's needed is a way to steam the crabs until they are cooked through.

1 dozen	live blue crabs
1/2 cup	Old Bay seasoning
	Bonus Butter (recipe follows), for serving

Prepare the steamer pot by adding a few inches of water to the bottom of the pot and placing it over high heat. Leave the chamber above it empty. Bring the bottom to a full boil. Once the bottom is boiling and the top chamber is filled with steam, add the crabs to the top, layering them in and coating them all generously with Old Bay. It's a personal thing, but I tend to go heavy on the seasoning. (If you're making a bunch of crabs you don't want to be shy, so have a fresh can of seasoning on hand.) On high heat over a good burner, a dozen crabs can take

15 to 20 minutes to cook through and will turn bright red when done. If you're unsure if they're ready, crack one open to check. I always check the inside body meat area as it's the meatiest and usually the last part to cook. Serve with Bonus Butter, for dipping.

Bonus Butter

Makes a generous 1 cup butter

I serve this butter hot with all types of foods to dip in or drizzle over, but any recipe in this chapter can certainly take it. (I use salted cultured butter, but adding a little extra salt is a simple fix if you have unsalted.)

1/2 pound (2 sticks)	salted butter
2 to 3 Tbsps.	Fermented Pepper Paste (page 100) or sambal
1 Tbsp.	white miso
1	small shallot, thinly sliced
4	garlic cloves, grated
1 tsp.	grated fresh ginger

Melt the butter over medium-low heat in a small saucepan. Add the remaining ingredients and increase the heat until the butter starts bubbling slightly. Keep stirring and adjust the heat if it begins foaming. Constantly stirring will help, but lowering the heat is key. Once the shallot is soft and beginning to break down a bit, I reduce the heat and let it chill out and stay just warm until serving.

Simple Corn

Serves 8

You may have noticed when buying corn that it's often packed on ice, like it's a whole fish. That's a really good sign. Keeping it ice cold helps prevent the corn's natural sweet crispness from degrading.

Here, we're cooking the corn in its husk, which steams the kernels. One fun little extra I do is take the corn and potatoes out of the cooler that's keeping them warm and throw them onto the grill. Toasted, charred corn still in the husk is one of my favorite things to peel and eat in the summer. The smell alone is worth it. The potatoes take to a hot dry roasting quickly as well, but feel free to toss them in some oil first if you prefer.

 Potatoes

	kosher salt
	Old Bay seasoning
8	ears corn on the cob, in the husks
2 pounds	small red or golden potatoes
	Bonus Butter (page 119)

Fill a cooler or big steam pot with iced water and add a handful each of salt and Old Bay, to where the water tastes nice—a little salty, but nice. Add the corn and soak for a few hours.

When it's time to cook, drain the corn, but use some of that soaking liquid to fill the bottom of a large lobster-style steamer pot.

Then layer corn and potatoes into the top steam basket in a manner to allow for equal steam flow throughout. (Meaning: I leave

Continues on next page

Continued
from previous
page

some gaps and holes between the veggies to allow the steam to travel up and around everything.)

Steam for 10 to 15 minutes, depending on the size of your potatoes; keep an eye out and monitor the potatoes and corn separately. If the corn is good and sweet, it'll be done in just a minute. If it's starchier, make sure it's cooked all the way to the cob.

The potatoes are done when you can easily pierce them with a fork. As the cobs finish, I transfer them directly to a clean, dry, small insulated cooler, while the potatoes keep steaming. The cooler acts as a hot box, locking in the heat for some time. Some slow additional cooking will occur in the cooler, so if you're gonna let them hang for a couple hours, pull everything out of the steamer while al dente.

These babies are ready to go right out of the cooler if you want. Just dump them out onto the table with some crabs and you are in good shape my friend. Or keep them in the closed cooler and people can grab the hot food when they want. Serve with hot **Bonus Butter.**

Split-Crab Chile Bowl

Serves 2

Especially in North America, not a lot of folks are eating as much of the crab as we could be. Some of the most flavorful parts of the crab aren't the meat. In many cuisines around the world, cooks use the body of the crab and its insides to build a rich flavorful broth. That's what we do here: We'll eat the meat, but also have this beautiful thick sauce to coat it. For me, it would be a crime not to utilize the flavor-building potential in the crab's body.

2 Tbsps.	fat of choice (I use extra-virgin olive oil)
3	shallots, finely chopped
2	live blue crabs, split in half between the eyes
4	scallions, sliced into 1-inch batons
1-inch	knob fresh ginger, minced
5	garlic cloves, crushed and chopped
3 Tbsps.	Pepper Mix (page 285)
3 Tbsps.	Fermented Pepper Paste (page 100) or sambal
1/2 cup	white wine
1/2 cup	water
2 Tbsps.	white miso
3 Tbsps.	salted butter
	fresh chopped parsley, for garnish

Heat the fat in a large skillet or wok over medium-high heat. Add the shallots and sauté for a few minutes. Add the crabs, scallions, ginger, and garlic, allowing them to cook for a few minutes. Next add the pepper mix and pepper paste or sambal and stir constantly for a minute or two before hitting the mixture with the wine. Let the wine reduce for another minute.

Add the water, miso, and butter to the skillet. I often turn the heat up to high here and keep stirring or agitating the wok. The constant stirring and moving of the liquids will help cook the crab evenly and build a nice pan sauce. The crab is imparting major flavor to the liquid and essentially making a wonderful little crab stock in the pan. If it's getting a little dry and thick, hit it with a little more water to keep it saucy. I've been known to add more butter than the amount specified above, just saying. I'll even throw in a little of that Bonus Butter (page 119), why not! I usually serve this over hot rice noodles or fresh steamed rice, topped with fresh chopped parsley.

Crab Rolls

There are two types of people when it comes to eating crabs. Both are fine (not really). One type gets a half-dozen crabs in front of them, and they pick them all to make a big pile of crabmeat. When they're done picking they gorge themselves. The other type of person picks as they eat, cracking a claw, eating it, and cracking the next claw. That's the kind of person I am, because crabmeat is never going to be better than the instant it comes from the shell.

But I also really love crab rolls. If you're in a situation where you have a lot of crabs, you're done eating them as you go, and you have leftovers…this is when your pile-pickers are ready to shine. Bring them back to the table and try to fill a quart container with picked meat, so that everyone can have a nice crab roll.

1 pound	picked crabmeat (or meat from 2 to 3 whole crabs for each roll)
1/3 cup	Fermented Tartar Sauce (recipe follows)
1/4 cup	chopped fresh chives or mixed herbs, plus more for garnish
	Pepper Mix (see page 285)
1/2 tsp.	garlic powder
1/2 tsp.	onion powder
	lemon juice, to taste
	kosher salt
	salted butter
4	top-split buns, or your favorite style of hot dog roll

Mix the crabmeat, tartar sauce, chives, pepper mix, garlic powder, onion powder, and a squeeze of lemon juice (more if you like) together in a medium bowl to make a crab salad. Adjust the amount of tartar sauce and/or lemon juice until the salad is your desired consistency and taste. Season to taste with salt, and feel free to play around a little here; sometimes I add minced shallots or pickled onions.

Melt a little butter and brush the buns inside and out with butter, then toast both sides in a cast-iron skillet over medium-low heat until golden and delightful to the eye. Spoon crab salad into the buns and garnish with some more herbs if you like. I always eat two rolls!

Fermented Tartar Sauce

Makes 1 pint

I really like tartar sauce. In my mind, sometimes even bad tartar sauce is good. It's kind of like pizza in that way. Tartar sauce is briny, fatty, and has the tanginess of pickles and a little briny vinegar. It's simple to elevate it and make your own, to take the experience to the next level. It's hard to go back to the stuff in a plastic tube when you can make something like this.

1 lb	Persian cucumbers
	kosher salt, 1.5 percent by weight
2	fresh bay leaves, bruised
3	garlic cloves, peeled and crushed
1/2 tsp.	celery seed
1/2 tsp.	Pepper Mix (page 285)
About 1 cup	mayonnaise
1 Tbsp.	lemon juice
1/2 tsp.	Old Bay Seasoning (optional)

Cut and crush the cucumbers into bite-size or smaller chunks. Weigh the cucumbers, then measure out 1.5 percent of that weight in kosher salt.

Toss the cucumbers with the salt, bay leaves, garlic, celery seed, and pepper mix in a medium bowl. Place the mixture into a vacuum bag or fermentation vessel of your choice and let ferment at room temperature for 3 to 4 days, until the cukes start to soften and wilt out some water.

Discard the bay leaves and drain the mixture, reserving both the cucumbers and the liquid. Chop the cucumbers into whatever texture you desire, then fold into the mayo. I recommend adding more mayo and fermented brine a little at a time to get the texture you'd prefer. Stir in the lemon and Old Bay. Store in the fridge for a few days.

A proper male blue claw crab

Tomato Love

6

Some folks don't like tomatoes and I have a theory as to why that might be. Here's a scenario: A kid walks into a deli and gets his favorite sandwich, but this time he gets tomatoes on it. He bites into the sandwich and within seconds the poorly sliced, underripe tomato is pulled off and hanging from his mouth. From that point forward, this kid will no longer order tomatoes on his sandwich. Another day, he tries the cucumber and tomato salad as a side dish, and again the tomatoes are a disappointment: mealy and flavorless. This kid will avoid tomatoes completely now and a tomato hate is born. It's unfortunate.

A huge percentage of tomatoes available to people at supermarkets or restaurants just aren't very good. Sure, it might *look* like a tomato on the outside. But time and time again the consumer tries to enjoy tomatoes and is disappointed. They purchase what they think (and hope) is a plump, ripe, and juicy specimen. Once at home, they cut into that out-of-season commodity and it has a white core, lacks flavor, and sports a texture that is equally sad. Strike out! If that's your experience with tomatoes, eventually you just stop buying them or grow to accept the poor quality.

There's a reason behind this sad situation. Tomatoes are generally grown somewhere far away and picked prematurely to maintain safe transport. They're stored in climate-controlled, gas-filled warehouses to prevent rotting while they await further shipment. And this old trick isn't limited to tomatoes. Avocados and bananas suffer the same fate so that consumers can enjoy tropical fruit year-round. We're all guilty of subscribing to and benefiting from this process. My kids in New Jersey love bananas every time of year, and I've gotten accustomed to cooking with the world at my fingertips. The access we have to all kinds of ingredients is an amazing feat of consumerism and science. But there are drawbacks. Food is often underripe, poorly textured, heavily shipped, and definitely not local and fresh.

The modern mass industrialization of our food supply isn't the focus of this chapter, but it is a reminder why I love tomatoes so much. I anticipate their natural growing season. I grew up with a small garden on the sunny side of the house. Mom kept the yard nice with

flowers and all that jazz and my dad managed the vegetables. It was a hobby of theirs. (I was always more drawn to the veggies because I've always been a little chowhound.) We grew lettuce, zucchini, string beans, eggplant, herbs, okra, and huge tomato plants. When I say huge, it's not just because I was a small boy and they seemed gigantic. Tomatoes grow on vines and some can get well over 6 feet if you take care of them right, and my ole man took good care of them!

Every night after a long day of work (sometimes two shifts), he'd drag the hose across the deck to the side of the house and stand there watering, sometimes in the dark. "Soak it good." The plants would run up long wooden stakes we drove into the ground. We tied the plant to the post and pruned it as it grew. It taught me patience and care; a lot of work went into those plants.

If you can, I highly recommend growing your own. All you need is a 5-gallon bucket and some sunlight. I grew them on the roof outside my window in a shared multifamily house in Brooklyn at one point. But if you can't, or aren't inclined to, I suggest you find some farmers' market near you and go *in season*. You'll know when it's tomato season because they will be everywhere and tomato nuts like me will race to the markets early to find the best ones.

Talking about tomato plants reminds me of another part of the tomato I love, besides the actual fruit (yes, fruit): *the leaves*. They produce a smell I wish *everyone* could experience; a pleasant, sweet, floral aroma that's simply unique. It's like catnip for me. Once I started my own garden, I invented a way to capture this fragrance and put it to use. I collect the recently pruned leaves and soak them in vinegar or salt to infuse and capture that amazing smell. Then I season meats and veggies with it or even use it to dress a salad.

Tomatoes are incredibly versatile. They come in so many different shapes, colors, and sizes and are such a treat, from super-sweet cherry or grape tomatoes that can be popped into your mouth like candy, to monster heirlooms you could cut thick and eat like a steak. Most of the time prep is best done simply, with tomatoes served at room temperature. Just put a little extra-virgin olive oil and some salt on them and you have an appetizer I'd buy any day.

Think simple! A little fresh basil and some good mozzarella cheese...amazing. It's all about the ingredients. When cooking simply, I can't stress enough the importance of getting the very best you can afford, grow, or find.

Have technology and indoor organic growth operations made the supermarket option a hell of a lot better than when I was a kid? Absolutely, and I'm grateful in many ways. But is it actually good for us that I can get a not-so-great fresh tomato year-round? I don't think so. What I do know is that waiting for ripe tomatoes that grow locally and are harvested off a vine is an experience I truly value. Every year in the Northeast when August comes, the big fat tomatoes start to pop up all over. After not seeing them for a whole year, it's a reason to celebrate. That celebration brings food, people, seasonality, and nature back together.

Would I have a passionate love for great tomatoes if they were available everywhere or all year long? It's hard to say. Maybe not, because love is always a little stronger when you can miss it. So, I continue to anxiously await the bursting tomato season every year, savoring it for the month or two it lasts. Join me?

All shapes and sizes. I simply love tomatoes.

Fermented

Serves 4

I love Bloody Marys, always have. I've had ones I can't finish and ones I dream about often.

For an arsenal of garnishes, you can pickle carrots, celery with leaves, olives, and small mushrooms the day before by soaking them all in vinegar with celery seed, fennel, and peppercorns. Or you can buy your favorite local pickles and accoutrements!

Bloody Mary Base

2 pounds	cherry tomatoes
40 grams	grated fresh horseradish root
3	garlic cloves, crushed and peeled
1/2 tsp.	Brad's Za'atar (page 227) or store-bought
15 grams	kosher salt

Continued
from previous
page

Combine **all of the ingredients** in a vacuum bag or a jar and allow to ferment at room temperature for 3 days or up to a week, until bubbly and the tomatoes begin to burst. I've gone pretty long with these at room temperature (like 2 weeks) in a vac bag and they were absolutely delicious.

Once all the tomatoes have burst, they are good to strain. Discard the solids. All the liquid you get is the base for your Bloody Mary. Store it in the fridge and consume it ASAP. If you forget about it or don't want to drink it anymore, poach some fish or chicken in it with a dab of butter...it's unbelievably good.

Tomato
Burrata
Life

The love story of tomatoes and creamy mozzarella is classic and timeless. Here, I give it a little switcheroo. I grew up with crusty Italian bread heavily seeded with sesame; adding toasted sesame seeds to this salad brings that familiar flavor and adds some crunch. I also like to complement basil with another herb, such as tarragon or my favorite, perilla. Perilla is not in the sesame family—it's closer to mint, horticulturally speaking—but perilla seeds and the plant itself kind of look and act like sesame to me. They all go well together. Adding a side of nice bread or some pizza won't be a bad plan either.

4	large tomatoes
	kosher salt (or the finishing salt of your choice)
	Pepper Mix (page 285)
1-pound ball	burrata
	extra-virgin olive oil
	fresh basil and tarragon, or basil and perilla
1 Tbsp.	toasted sesame seeds

Cut the tomatoes into rounds about 1/2 inch thick and layer them around a big platter. I like to chill the platter first; crazy, but I do it. Season the fruit with your favorite salt and the pepper mix. Place the cheese ball in the center of the tomatoes and drizzle everything generously with top-shelf medical-grade extra-virgin olive oil. Yes, medical grade. I made that designation up, but you know what I mean—the good stuff, spicy and pungent. Garnish with herbs and sesame seeds and cut open that cheese ball when you present the salad at the table. Eat as much as you can while these fruits are in peak season!

Sunday Sauce and Gravy

Makes 3 quarts

Is it tomato "gravy" or "sauce"? My parents taught me that the only difference was that gravy had meat cooked in it. Mom would throw in a browned bone-in pork chop, sausages and meatballs, braciole, shanks, ribs, neck bones…you can use whatever you can get/got/want! I always got in trouble sneaking out the meatballs throughout the day.

Whatever you call it, it's all about the tomatoes here. You can go down the fresh-tomato rabbit hole if you want to. I've grown and milled my own tomatoes for sauce and had both good and bad results; growing your own food can be hard. That said, the year I nailed homegrown tomato farming, the sauce I made was unbelievable. It made me want to grow an acre's worth for vats of sauce to jar and lock in the flavors to enjoy all year-round. Tweaking the

varieties you use in a sauce to meet your preferred acid and sugar levels is fun. Do that if you want, it's worth it. Or you can just buy your favorite canned tomatoes. I really love Bianco DiNapoli crushed or whole organic tomatoes—a personal preference. If you find a good company that cares and gets it right, they'll have already done what I describe above for you!

Here's a base recipe that's inspired by the sauce my mom made in large amounts and froze for future quick-but-homemade meals. I have to call it sauce, but to make it gravy, just cook some damn meat in it, and don't call it sauce anymore. Or, take a peek at the bonus recipe at the end of the Blue Crab chapter intro (page 116) and throw some crabs in there.

Sunday Sauce

1/2 cup	extra-virgin olive oil
1/2 to 1	shallot, thinly sliced
5	garlic cloves, thinly sliced
1	anchovy
1/4 cup	white wine
1/4 cup	red wine
4 large (28-ounce)	cans tomatoes (milled, diced, whole—your call)
	small chunks peeled sweet potato (definitely optional and highly controversial)
	kosher salt and ground black pepper, to taste
3 Tbsps.	salted butter
4	fresh bay leaves
2 sprigs	fresh oregano
2 sprigs	fresh basil

Sunday Gravy

your choice of meat, as much or as little as you like
extra-virgin olive oil

To make the sauce: Heat the oil in a large heavy saucepan over medium-high heat for 1 minute. Add the shallot, garlic, and anchovy and cook for (seriously) just 20 seconds. Then hit the pan with the white and red wine and let it simmer for a few minutes over high heat. Add the tomatoes and highly controversial sweet potato chunks, if using, and reduce the heat to medium. Season with salt and pepper and stir thoroughly.

Let the sauce simmer for hours over low heat. The sauce should never burn on the bottom! Taste it often, stir it, and stop simmering whenever you want!

About 30 minutes before the sauce is done, I like to stir in the butter and herbs and give it one last check for seasoning. I love to freeze quarts of it and defrost it to make pizzas or pasta or whatever.

To make gravy: Before making the sauce, sprinkle your meat of choice with salt and brown it in some olive oil in the large heavy saucepan you'll make sauce in. Remove the meat and set it aside, then do everything described above for the sauce. When you think the meat has time to cook properly before the sauce is done, add it to the sauce and cook until done. Large, bone-in cuts need more time than sausage links. If you plan to cook it all day, just keep watching it.

Spicy
Smoked

Tomato
Chicken

Served hot or cold, you can't beat this smoked chicken. What stands out about it is the fermented tomato, which has an earthy sweetness and funkiness. As it caramelizes onto the chicken skin with the chicken fat and spices, it becomes a salty, fatty, sweet tomato jam that creeps into all the crevasses of the meat and is unbelievably delicious.

Smoke the bird if you can—if you're looking for perfection—but this recipe works just fine with an oven roasted bird. I like to split the chicken in half because I love how it opens the cavity and exposes the insides to the heat and smoke, letting it cook more quickly and take on more flavor. But go ahead and use a whole chicken or chicken parts, it doesn't matter. In fact, I really enjoy making this recipe with thighs or drumsticks.

Fermented Tomato Base

1 pound	cherry tomatoes
2 sprigs	fresh thyme
1	habanero chile, seeded
3	garlic cloves, crushed and peeled
1/2 tsp.	Pepper Mix (page 285)
1 tsp.	kosher salt

One 3- to 4-pound	whole chicken, split (salted 1 day ahead)
	kosher salt
	extra-virgin olive oil

Glaze

1/2 cup	Fermented Tomato Base (above)
1/2 cup	honey
1/4 cup	extra-virgin olive oil
2 Tbsps.	mirin
2 Tbsps.	soy sauce (I used shoyu)
1 Tbsp.	Pepper Mix (page 285)
3 sprigs	fresh thyme

Sauce

1/2 cup	Fermented Tomato Base (above)
1/4 cup	extra-virgin olive oil
1 tsp.	Brad's Za'atar (page 227) or store-bought

To start the fermented tomato base: Combine all the base ingredients in a vacuum bag or a fermentation vessel (jar, crock, or bag). I prefer the vacuum bag for this ferment because it prevents oxidation, which changes the tomatoes' color and flavor. I like the mixture to finish bright red, not a shade of rust. Let the mixture ferment

Continues on next page

Continued
from previous
page

at room temperature for a few days or up to a week, until the tomatoes are all busted up and juicy. Like most ferments this will be affected by the temperature of the environment it's fermenting in. A hot room makes for a faster ferment, but in my opinion that doesn't always mean a better ferment.

I like to break the tomatoes up with my fingers throughout the process, but that will also happen on its own over time too. Once nice and juicy, I pour the base into a blender and pulse until smooth. This is optional. I don't like to strain out that fiber, I've found it helps make a better sauce and glaze, but please fool around here! After blending, I divide the base in half, one half for the glaze and one half for the sauce.

For the glaze: Stir all the glaze ingredients together in a medium bowl.

For the sauce: Stir all the sauce ingredients together in a medium bowl.

Like the larger cuts of meat I cook, I salt the chicken for this dish 24 hours before I cook it. Salting ahead will make for a juicier bird that's nicely seasoned all the way to the bone. Simply rub the bird inside and out, under the skin and all over with kosher salt—about 1 tsp. per pound of meat. Wrap and refrigerate it.

When you're ready to cook, preheat the smoker or oven to 225°F.

Give the salted bird a light coating of oil before placing it split-side down in the smoker or in a roasting pan and placing it in the oven. Let cook for about an hour before starting to brush on the glaze. I apply with a brush about every 40 minutes until the chicken reaches an internal temperature of 160°F, a total of about 3–4 hours.

At that point, I crank the temp up to 400°F and brush on more glaze every 5 minutes or so, to allow the sugars to begin to caramelize and build a nice sticky glazed surface. This should take just about 10 minutes longer: The outside should be sticky and caramelized and taste like a spicy tomato jam. Don't get distracted and walk away from the smoker at this point; you've worked days and hours to make this dish and you can ruin it by letting it burn in the final minutes.

Once the joints of the bird are loose and the internal temperature is about 170°F, I remove it from the oven or smoker and let it rest. Slice and serve with the fermented sauce.

Tomato and

Makes 4 to 6 servings

This is an easy salad to whip up fast
without sacrificing quality. Don't rinse the
canned beans unless the liquid is really
thick—the remaining liquid that clings to
the beans will help thicken the dressing
slightly.

Bean Salad

1 pound	mixed cherry tomatoes, halved
1 (15.5-ounce) can	white beans, drained (I use butterbeans or cannellini, the best quality I can get)
1	shallot, minced
2 Tbsps.	white miso
2 cups	bite-size chunks cucumber
	kosher salt
	Pepper Mix (page 285)
1/4 cup	extra-virgin olive oil
1/4 cup	toasted sunflower seeds
	dried or fresh oregano

I literally put everything in a big bowl or
bag and toss well for a minute to build a
nice saucy salad. It's great cold or at room
temperature and pairs well with just about
any grilled meal.

BLTs

Makes 4 sandwiches

When the tomatoes are perfect, it's the best time of year to satisfy that BLT craving.

I'm not going to start by saying you need thick-cut bacon…use whatever you have or want. Sometimes I like bacon 1/4 inch thick and sometimes I like crispy thin slices. I like to make sourdough bread (page 153) for my BLTs; I enjoy it toasted and sliced on the thicker side. But use any bread you'd like.

What I *am* going to say is to get yourself some beautiful, vine-ripened tomatoes from a garden or farmers' market. I like to compare the magic of a BLT to that of a PB&J sandwich: simple with just a couple of ingredients. Use the absolute best ingredients you can get and it will turn this simple meal into a masterpiece to remember and be excited for.

for Dinner

Continues on
next page

Continued
from previous
page

1 pound	sliced bacon
	Pepper Mix (page 285)
2 cloves	roasted garlic (see page 336)
	Mayonnaise
8 slices	sourdough, rye, or white bread
2	large ripe tomatoes, sliced
	lettuce, your call here on what type

Cook the bacon till crispy, I usually use it sliced on the thinner side and cooked until crispy to the point where it starts to shatter a little. For me that's perfect for a BLT, but it's 100 percent a personal preference and I'm cool with that. I like to cook the bacon on a wire rack set in a sheet pan in a 400°F oven.

Don't ask for a specific cooking time…just keep an eye on it as specific ovens, bacon types, and thicknesses will cause variations in cook times. (If you can't tell already, I hate specific cook times, ha.)

Mix pepper mix and roasted garlic into mayo. (I prefer Hellmann's on a BLT, because I think the pink peppercorn and roasted garlic go so well with it, but you can make your own mayo or use Duke's or a local favorite.)

I'm not gonna explain a BLT anymore. Just use the best ingredients you can. Love BLTs? Then grow some tomatoes or spend some time finding the perfect ones. Make it a tradition and ritual to adore! Even simple things like BLTs deserve respect and celebration.

Brad's Sourdough + Starter Baby Child Love

Makes enough for 8 (250-gram) balls of pizza dough or flatbread, or 2 boules or 1 large loaf

I use this sourdough to make all types of breads like pizza, loaves, boules, and flatbreads. I'm no master of bread by any means, but highly encourage you to go down this simple and extremely complex cooking adventure by checking out books of knowledge from people who have devoted lifetimes to it. There are thousands of bread variations from every corner of the world, bread is life…so definitely try those too!

These are my numbers and notes that allow me to re-create this magical and ancient process, but to be honest, I no longer use a recipe for reference and instead riff on the guidance and

Continues on next page

Continued from previous page

numbers here. I have experimented with flours and percentages and have made a ton of horrible baked carbohydrate products that I can't even call bread. It can get tricky with different flours and hydrations, but the baseline here gives me amazing results when I don't screw it up or experiment. Take your own notes, and if you're interested, search out more detailed information from the true experts. Some of the books that have inspired me are the Tartine books from Chad Robertson and Elisabeth Prueitt and *Pizza Camp* by Joe Beddia. The internet is helpful as well, and in-person classes and workshops are priceless in my opinion. Keep at it. You will get better every time. It's beautiful.

Making and eating bread with wild yeast that I have collected and nurtured, dough that I've kneaded and baked, and then sharing it with friends and family is one of my favorite food-related activities. It connects us both to each other and to our food. It always reminds me how far we have gotten away from our food systems. Something as common and simple as making and eating homemade bread has become rare for a lot of families. My parents didn't make bread. They made lots of things from scratch, but never bread and certainly not sourdough. Being a parent now, having my kids ask me, "When are you making bread again, Daddy? It's so good," reminds me how important these common foods are.

To make naturally leavened sourdough, you first need to build a starter. Here's how:

Starter (7 Days)

Day 1—In a quart jar, mix together 25 grams water and 25 grams good-quality bread flour. Cover the top with cheesecloth and let sit at room temperature out of the sun.

Day 2—"Feed" the starter in the jar by stirring in equal amounts flour and water: 25 grams water and 25 grams flour.

Day 3—Feed again with 25 grams water and 25 grams flour.

Day 4—Remove and discard (or save for another use) 100 grams of the starter. Feed the remaining starter with 50 grams water and 50 grams flour.

Day 5—Remove 100 grams of the starter. Feed the remaining starter again with 50 grams water and 50 grams flour.

Day 6—By now, the starter should be bubbly and growing in volume. Feed and bulk it up by adding 150 grams water and 150 grams flour.

Day 7—Pull off the starter you want to use to bake—the recipe below calls for 150 grams. Feed the starter left in the jar with 50 grams water and 50 grams flour.

At this point, unless I'm baking bread daily, I cover my starter with a lid and store it in the fridge. I feed it equal parts flour and water two or three times a week, but it can survive longer without feeding if needed. A starter should be airy and active but slow and complex when in the fridge. A little liquid may form on the surface, especially during long unfed periods. Like any other fermentation, it should smell a little funky, but get rid of it if it smells really nasty or you see black or pink mold.

Dough

1,000 grams total flours (but using 100 percent all-purpose flour will work too):

    700 grams   bread flour
    150 grams   rye flour
    150 grams   fine Italian flour (type "00")

750 grams filtered, room-temperature water (for 75 percent hydration)
25 grams fine salt
30 grams extra-virgin olive oil
150 grams starter, airy and fed the night before

This recipe makes a lot of dough, and the instructions below show you how to make one loaf of sourdough bread and four balls of pizza dough. But it's just dough! You could make two loaves, or eight balls of dough, or several dozen garlic knots. This is just a solid workhorse dough that you can develop and mature into your own style.

Sift and mix the flours together in a bowl—just the flours—then mix in the water. (Use filtered water if you can; I've used city tap water and it worked, but with a long, careful process like bread making I don't want to risk using iffy water.) Cover the bowl and allow the flour and water to sit together for a while. This is called autolyze; definitely do it as it will help with your gluten development big time. The mixture will look shaggy and nothing like the dough you want it to become, but it's important to make sure all the flour is beginning to hydrate from the water added. I've let the autolyze go on for anywhere from 30 minutes to 30 hours, covered or not, both successfully. (But do cover the bowl, as not doing so could be a mistake. Valuable info.)

When the flour is completely hydrated and elastic in one mass, add the salt, oil, and starter to the flour and water mixture. I use my hands to fold all this together, then begin kneading the mixture into a smooth and uniform ball of dough. Fold and knead and gently stretch. I do a little slap-and-fold move I got comfortable with. I do this for a few minutes before covering the dough with plastic wrap and allowing it to begin fermenting. Leave it at room temperature—warmer equals faster fermentation.

During the first 30 to 90 minutes, I do a set of turns and folds, or stretches as I call them. I pick the dough up and let it stretch down under its own weight, then put it down,

Continues on next page

Continued
from previous
page

folding it under itself, gentle and beautiful. Imagine picking up a scarf and slowly putting it down to create nice layers in the fabric.

Then I let the dough bulk ferment for a few hours to double in volume. I do two more folds during this time too, rotating the dough a quarter-turn first, and being very careful not to deflate all the fermented gas bubbles inside the dough. I keep the dough in a lightly oiled square container or steel bowl and wet my hands before each handling.

This is an all-day tending activity that can go to hell if not done with love and attention. Bread: Easy to make, difficult to make well.

When the bulk fermentation is done (overnight, usually), I dust the table with flour and gently scrape the dough out onto the surface. Lightly flour everything you touch, including a bench scraper for cutting the dough in half. It's time to shape and place the dough into bowls lined with towels and dusted with flour; have the bowls prepared before you start touching the dough or shaping it.

Bread is life.

To Make Bread

Divide the dough in half. Reserve one half for making balls of pizza dough. Shape the other half and flip it into a basket so the finished end or top of loaf is facing down. Cover with plastic and place in the fridge overnight. The next day, preheat the oven to 500°F with a covered Dutch oven inside. Remove the dough from the fridge and flip gently onto a lightly floured sheet of parchment paper. Make the desired cuts on top to release steam. Place the dough

Long sourdough Pullman. One of my favorite types of bread to make.

on the paper right into Dutch oven, paper and all. Cover the Dutch oven with the lid and place it back in the oven. Turn the temperature down to 460°F and bake for 20 to 25 minutes. This will steam the bread. Remove the lid and bake for another 40 to 45 minutes, until the outside is a nice dark preferred color you're looking for. If you pick it up and thump the bottom with a knuckle, it should sound hollow, not dense. Like you trapped air in bread, not wet sticky dough. Let the bread rest on a rack for an hour before eating.

To Make Pizza Dough

Cut the second half of the dough into four equal pieces and shape into pizza balls. I do this by folding the dough in on itself with my fingers until it becomes a ball, then pinching the bottom. Place in small bowls with a light dusting of flour. Cover and refrigerate overnight. (You don't need to do this second refrigeration, but I recommend it for depth of flavor. You can also freeze the dough at this stage if desired, or the next morning as well.) The next day, before making pizza, let the dough proof at room temperature for a couple of hours. Lightly flour the dough and surface before working the dough into pizza crusts and baking.

Low tide, Maine

Vacationland

7

I've had a love affair with the state of Maine my whole life, and I'm sure as hell not the only one. Their license plate reads "Vacationland" and I've yet to call bullshit on that, because summers in Maine are absolutely perfect. Sure, the winters are long and harsh, but there's a quiet beauty in that too. The long fading days of summer are my favorite: hot during the day and cool at night. It's the perfect recipe to get outside all day and then enjoy a backyard fire and lower temps at night...and great sleeping weather!

I try to head up to Maine at least once every summer. The allure is no secret, as hot summers across the East Coast send tons of visitors to upper New England to enjoy more comfortable weather. And people aren't the only ones seeking refuge from the warmer temps of the south. From Maine's land to its coastal ocean waters, cooler temperatures allow everything from microorganisms to large predators to flourish and feed.

On a recent trip to a small coastal town in Maine, about 3 hours north of Portland, I met up with my friend Evan. He has spent lots of time in the area and was going to help me navigate this new and beautiful spot. Upon arrival, I was greeted with large baskets of chanterelles and black trumpet mushrooms that Evan had picked up on the way over. I'll never forgive myself for not taking pictures of that bounty. Evan, I'm sorry and it still stings. I'll take it as an incentive to continue to take long walks in the woods, where there's so much opportunity to find small edible plants and berries.

Foraging is the best: such a fun and easy way to get out into the woods and enjoy the bounty of what nature provides. With that said, I can't stress the importance of accessing an expert like Evan when you start exploring edible wild items. It seems obvious, but please never eat anything unless you are 1,000 percent sure what it is. Also, you need to know the time of year when you can eat/harvest items—it matters! Really, it's just fun to walk, learn, and try to identify what you are seeing, even without eating.

Enough about the woods. The reason I came up to Maine was for the water. The Maine shoreline is awe inspiring; at some points the shoreline is rocky and forest-edged while other areas are sandy and as clear as the Mediterranean. From Cadillac Mountain, the highest eastern coastal peak, where the sunlight first kisses America, to the blue-blooded reputation of southern beach points like Kennebunkport, the coast is amazing. Aside from its visual beauty, Maine waters are bountiful and well cared for. There's fantastic diversity and delicious offerings. You just need to keep an open mind and take the time to learn to look in the right places.

In this chapter I want to focus on two very different types of Maine seafood: shellfish and seaweed.

Clammin'

Maine's coastline is a puzzle of channels, coves, tributaries, bays, and islands. Take a look at a map and you'll see that there is actually more shoreline in Maine than California (Maine's tidal shoreline comes in at 3,478 miles compared to California's 3,427). And the ocean tidal swings are BIG! When the tide goes out, the water retreats way back toward the sea, exposing giant mud beds. These flats are where some of my favorite seafood lives and it's all right under your feet.

We started off digging in the mud flats and wading in small tidal pools looking for different types of shellfish. Armed with a clamming rake and wooden basket, Evan and I hit a few spots looking for razor clams and steamers. Both are rather tricky to find and require a bit of hard (but fun) work. Start in low tide, on those mud flats where the water has receded, and look for little holes in the mud where air bubbles find their way to the surface. Different clams have different looking mud holes, and you get to know what to look for.

Razor clams:

If I had to guess, the razor clam got its name because the shell looks like an old-school straight-edge razor and it's sharp as hell. These bad boys dig and run in the mud rather quickly, so you really need to be fast and ready. I'm not kidding, it's hard work—but when you do catch one, it's a fantastic sense of accomplishment…and that sweet and tender clam will be the best one you've ever eaten—either steamed with butter, or raw with some lime, togarashi, and olive oil, or whatever your fancy.

Razor clams

Steamers

Steamer or "pissah" clams:

You know the ones that have the very phallic and ugly looking tube that's wrapped in a very unattractive skin hanging out of the shell? Well, that's our guy! Get past the visual ugliness and these babies are the best. Creamy, sweet, and an absolute treat steamed up and served with clam broth and butter. Pop them out of the shell, peel off that unattractive skin, splash it in the broth to wash off any last sand, then finish in the butter. I crave them all year. Steamers are easily one of my favorite seafoods. These guys don't run as fast in the mud, but they have very soft shells that can break easily. It happens to the best of us, so be careful!

Tidal pool explorations

We couldn't eat everything we dug up that day due to red tides, toxic levels in the water from algae growth and other imbalances. It happens and isn't that uncommon. These conditions are closely monitored and reported for recreational and commercial shellfishing. Always check the local regulations and warnings because there can be a very serious health risk to the consumer or gatherer. Again, pay attention and cross check!

This toxic tide threw a curveball in this trip, but hey, that's life. We safely returned what we harvested back to the sea...a bummer, but I'll be back! Luckily, my buddy Will runs a seafood business out of Portland. He pulled through and met us at the house with a cooler full of beautiful razor clams, true littleneck clams, steamers, and oysters. Any healthy oyster is a good oyster, but in my opinion, Maine oysters are the best. It was a great ending to a great day even though we didn't keep what we gathered. We spent the day learning, exploring, digging, and running from the tides like little boys in the late summer sun. Hard work and fun rounded out with a home run of a dinner? That's a Good Maine Day.

Lobster

The next morning, we woke up and hopped in cars to travel north a couple hours to get on a lobster boat. We wanted to pull some traps and bring back our next meal. Maine is famous for producing the most lobsters in America, and some claim the best. There are roughly 10,000 lobstermen in the state of Maine, where it's generally a family business and licenses are limited in an effort to sustain a healthy lobster population. We met up with a few guys in the trade, and they entertained us with stories and taught us about their work. The older, more experienced lobsterman was showing a younger guy the ropes. Even though we had only a short glimpse, their conversations about water routes, inland operations, hazards, and the hundreds of regulations around lobster fishing clued us in to how knowledgeable these fishermen are.

Many lobster outfits run private tours on their boats during the off-season. A few years back when vacationing in Old Orchard Beach with my family, we took a tour like this out of Portland. We learned about the importance of sustainable lobster fishing, how to measure them and determine which are "keepers." My niece and nephew (probably ages 9 and 7 at the time) pulled in traps and donned orange rubber overalls. We bought all the lobsters we caught (for a very reasonable price) and feasted that night. I highly recommend these excursions as they help support the local economy while teaching families about this important and difficult job.

You can get as fancy as you want with lobster, but I'm more of a purist. I like to keep it classic most of the time, simply steaming them with butter and lemon. With any extra (as if there will be leftovers), make some lobster salad, lobster rolls (hot or cold), or add the meat to mashed potatoes, potato salad, or mac and cheese.

Seaweed

I think "seaweed" as a blanket term misrepresents the value of sea plants. They're not weeds, just as a dandelion is an edible, delicious plant when used correctly. The idea of eating and consuming sea plants or "weeds" is nothing new in many cultures. There are many varieties, and I believe they are an underutilized natural resource.

Atlantic sugar kelp and dulse are the seaweeds that I use most in the kitchen. The kelp is defined by long, leathery, dark green ribbons that poetically flow in the water with the currents, maybe grabbing your legs as you swim. The dulse is a finer, bright purple sea plant whose beauty reminds me more of tropical vegetation you'd find on a reef while snorkeling.

These varieties are high in vitamins and minerals. The plants themselves require no watering, fertilization, or maintenance, and most varieties grow very quickly with high yields—they have begun to be farmed by fishermen and lobstermen during the off-season. Did I mention they absorb carbon from the environment? On top of all that, seaweed is wonderful to cook with. It can be consumed fresh, cooked, or dried. You can dehydrate it easily, storing for months if not years.

Checking lobsters for keeper size

Harvesting sugar kelp

How the heck do you cook with seaweed besides soup or salad? I hear this question often and I always encourage folks to look at these ingredients as umami or salt enhancers with flavor as deep as the ocean—use them dried in spice blends, add to your favorite dressings, or throw into braises, stews, and soups. The recipe on page 195 for cured fish with miso and kelp is by far one of my favorite fish preparations to make—it's so good and easy. But I didn't invent that, it's a riff on a traditional Japanese method that I first learned with sablefish (aka black cod). In fact, many Asian cultures weave sea vegetables into their cooking. They are a natural resource around the world to people who live in and around coastal areas.

I hope you will give sea plants a chance if you aren't already a fan. Hell, if you live by the ocean, go get a book about it and forage for yourself. It can be a great activity to get kids outdoors and involved in their food. You'd be surprised what kids will eat when they "catch it" themselves.

I wasn't successful in harvesting much by way of sea plants on this trip to Maine, as it was not the ideal time of year. But being able to get out into the water with friends and get my hands dirty digging up and harvesting foods is something that I will always love. It's an activity I catch myself daydreaming about. I'd certainly love to make it an annual tradition to harvest my year's supply of magical sea vegetables by getting in the water and mud flats with my kids.

Wild Maine sea grass and seaweed

Mixed Shellfish

in a Wok

Serves 2

The broth that this dish creates is what life is all about. Although you could cook the shellfish with bacon to add another layer of flavor, most of the time I don't because it's too much—but sometimes I'll add in a little miso. If you can get your hands on some lovage, try it here. An underrated, underutilized, hardy herb that pairs phenomenally with shellfish, lovage is like if parsley and celery leaves had a baby.

In this recipe, I love that the wok becomes a serving vessel—but because it has the sloped walls, you can get into it easier than a straight-sided pot. And on top of it being a great serving vessel, the wok is a workhorse for cooking over fire. It's large, light, and gets hot fast.

1/4 cup	extra-virgin olive oil
1	shallot, sliced
2	shiitake mushroom caps, thinly sliced
2	garlic cloves, sliced
1 tsp.	grated fresh ginger
2 dozen	littleneck clams, steamers, oysters, or mussels, scrubbed
1/2 cup	sake or white wine
2 Tbsps.	salted butter
1 cup	fresh lovage or parsley leaves, whole or chopped

grilled bread and butter
Fermented Pepper Paste (page 100) or sambal, if you're feeling the heat
steamed white rice topped with Brad's Furikake (page 192, optional)

Set a wok over medium-high heat and add the olive oil. When it's hot and shimmering, add the shallot and mushrooms and cook for about 5 minutes, until they have sweated out and picked up a little color. Then add the garlic and ginger and cook for a minute longer. Add the clams or other shellfish right on top, then pour in the sake. Put the butter and herbs on top. Cover with the lid (or a blanket of seaweed) and let steam until the shellfish have opened.

Enjoy with bread and a spicy pepper paste like sambal. I also love to eat this with a side of steamed white rice topped with furikake.

Old Bay

Steamed Lobster

Lobster has a special place in my heart. It had to be a special day for my parents to buy us a couple lobsters—meaning it had to be disgustingly low-priced on sale somewhere. That seemed to happen at the end of summer. My dad would go down to a lobster pound and get the ones that only had one claw because they were cheaper.

Some people hate on lobster and say they're not as good as crabs, but I think that's because they aren't cooking them right. Or, they might be buying lobster with their ego, leaving with a 4-pound monster, when the truth is that the smaller ones taste better. Any real lobster eater knows you want to get the "chicks," the ones that weigh in at about a pound and a half.

Lobsters are special and you should treat them that way…even if they really are just big cockroaches.

5	live lobsters, 1½ to 2 pounds each
1 pound	baby red potatoes
1	onion, split in half
	handful garlic and fresh ginger, crushed whole cloves and chunks
	Old Bay seasoning, about 1/3 cup, but it's your call
	Bonus Butter (page 119), for serving (optional)

Add water to the biggest lobster pot you can get with a steamer basket or colander inside and bring to a ripping boil. If you don't have a lobster pot, anything that will steam something without boiling it will work. Get creative—I certainly have before. My folks always had a lobster pot and my dad brings it along on *every* vacation. Hell, he brings an oyster and clam knife too, just in case he ends up in that kinda jam.

Place the lobsters, potatoes, onion, and garlic and ginger in the basket. Sprinkle with Old Bay. Steam for about 13½ minutes, until the lobster is bright red. Sometimes coagulated white stuff will come out of the

Continues on next page

Continued
from previous
page

joints, and the tail will pull in and become rounded. You should be able to easily pierce the potatoes with a fork. Uncover and let sit for a few minutes before eating as they are ripping hot.

Or, if you like, while the lobsters steam, prepare an ice-water bath. Right after the hot steam, shock each lobster in the ice water for 30 seconds. This will help the meat-picking experience, allowing the meat to easily release from those tough shells. If you want to eat them cold or later, continue to chill them ASAP.

Serve the lobster with the potatoes and **Bonus Butter.**

I'd say that three-fifths of the times I eat lobster, I bleed from my hands and I'm okay with that. I prefer to use a single chopstick and some sharp, small kitchen shears. If done properly the claws will be full of the most perfect lobster broth one could make. I love to crack a claw off and then remove the pincer. I'll let you picture what I describe as a lobster soup shooter. It's one of my favorite things in life.

Scallop Crudo

with

Citrus and Chile

Serves 4

When it comes to seafood, the scallop is easy to get behind. It has a rich, dense texture that takes really well to raw preparations. And whenever you're dealing with raw preparations of any kind, you want to get the best possible ingredients you can, from the most trustworthy sources, as locally as possible. So, no, you wouldn't want to make this with a bag of frozen scallops. You can also use a really clean-tasting, firm white fish like fluke, striped bass, or black sea bass. You name it: The spiciness, the oiliness, and citrusy flavor profile lend themselves well to just about any type of raw seafood.

Chile Paste

2 Tbsps.	extra-virgin olive oil
2	habanero chiles, seeded
3	Fresno chiles, seeded
	slice of garlic (optional)
	grated zest of 1 grapefruit
	grated zest of 1 lime
	kosher salt, to taste

6	large dry sea scallops
	grapefruit or lime juice, to taste
2 Tbsps.	extra-virgin olive oil
1/4 cup	toasted pistachios, chopped
	chopped herbs, for garnish

For the chile paste: Place all the ingredients in a food processor or mortar and pestle and process or mash into a fine paste. You can use this right away, or put in a jar or bag and let it ferment at room temperature for a day or two.

When ready to serve, slice the scallops thin or thick, any way you want to eat them, and toss them in a medium bowl with the paste. Combine the citrus juice and oil in a shallow serving bowl. Place the scallops in the bowl and garnish with the pistachios and herbs.

Ocean Bomb

Make as many as you want

How many dozens of raw oysters can
you eat? After two or three dozen, that's
a lot of raw stuff in your belly. That's
when I start cooking these—they're what
a clam, mussel, or steamer wishes it
could be.

Grilled Oysters

oysters (as many as you like)
Bonus Butter (page 119), optional

Fire up a grill and place the oysters on racks
over the hot fire. I recommend placing the
shells with their cups (curved side) down so
that you don't lose any of the sweet and
perfectly hot oyster liquor. Wait till you start
to see some shells pop open just a little bit.
Some take longer than others. Take them
off the grill as they pop open and their juices
start to bubble.

Use an oyster knife to pop open the back
hinge, then sweep it under the adductor
muscle to release the meat. After that, just
be careful: They get hot but this is one of
my absolute favorite ways to enjoy oysters.
They're perfect and I hardly ever put
anything else on them, unless it's a little hot
Bonus Butter. But they don't need it. Nature
nailed it once again.

Pickled Mussels

Makes about 1 pint

Like our good friend the cold squid salad (page 82), pickled mussels aren't something I order out everywhere—so making them became a fun activity at home. When mussels are around, you can get a lot of them for cheap. That's good, because when you've got a half-dozen friends sitting around eating mussels and drinking wine, you don't want to run out. That also means you might wind up with some extras. The next day, when you're not drunk anymore, pick 'em and preserve 'em. They will keep in the fridge for a few days, but definitely consume within 5 days.

2 pounds	mussels, scrubbed
1/2 cup	extra-virgin olive oil
1/4 cup	thinly sliced leek greens
1	shallot, minced
	Pepper Mix (page 285), to taste
3	garlic cloves, thinly sliced
1 1/2 tsps.	smoked paprika
	nice pinch saffron (optional)
1/4 cup	champagne vinegar

Add a little water to a large steam pot and steam the mussels until they begin to open, a few minutes. Discard any mussels that don't open. Remove the meat from the shells and place the mussel meat and their liquid in a bowl.

In a small saucepan over low heat, combine the oil, leeks, shallot, and pepper and sweat for a minute. Add the garlic, paprika, and saffron and bloom in the oil for 30 seconds. Pour the hot oil over the mussels and stir in the vinegar. Serve hot, or chill in a jar for up to 5 days and serve at room temperature. This is great with some bread or a salad or over some rice for a quick dinner.

Dried Seaweed

Once you're comfortable finding or buying seaweeds, a great way to use them is to dry them in whole form to use that way, or powder them. I do both. Perfect for getting umami and that natural ocean-briny flavor into dishes. Seaweeds, loaded with minerals and other nutrients, are one of my favorite types of vegetation. Eat more seaweed!

Sugar kelp and dulse seaweeds are easy to use in soups and stews, or powdered and added to sauces and sausages. Use a dehydrator or just hang and let nature do its thing. Salt crystals will form on the outside as the seaweed dries and transforms into an amazing ingredient that's cheap and practical.

Seaweed has been a huge part of cultures and culinary dishes around the world because of how good it is for health and because it is so abundant in coastal areas. It may seem like a "new" food to some in the U.S., but large populations from other countries have always consumed it, and it's finally getting more attention here. Whether foraging for some or buying from a producer or farmer, seaweeds are a fun and engaging way to get into different foods and activities. I ask if you do go harvest your own seaweed, pick up and dispose of a piece of someone else's trash on every outing.

I gather seaweed and keep it wet with seawater in a bag until it is time to dry and process the haul. I wash it gently and then hang it to dry. If I want to eat it fresh, then I keep it in a container with some seawater I took from the ocean. I quickly rinse it with fresh water right before serving.

Bonus thought: Fish sausage with seaweed. This is a fun little aside to inspire you. Putting different dried seaweeds into fish or meat sausages can give you really interesting and delicious outcomes. It can help with flavor and contributes a curing agent in the form of naturally occurring sodiums.

Examining sugar kelp
blades

Air-drying dulse and
sugar kelp

Brad's Furikake

Makes about 3/4 cup

Furikake is a common table condiment
and topper in Japanese cuisines
that comes in many variations, but
most have a few things in common,
including dried nori, toasted sesame
seeds, salt, and spices. If you make
your own, it can be a blank canvas
for your own creative ingredients and
flavor profiles. Furikake for life!

1/4 cup	crumbled dried kelp
1/4 cup	crumbled dried dulse
1/4 cup	toasted sesame seeds
2 Tbsps.	dried perilla (optional, I grow it and cut the leaves into chiffonades to dry)
1 tsp.	crumbled dehydrated garlic kosher salt
1 tsp.	sugar
1/4 tsp.	dehydrated grated lime zest (for optional zing)
	pepper flakes or cayenne (for optional heat)

Just go ahead and add everything to
a jar and mix it together. Seal and store.
You'll end up using it on everything,
from eggs to congee.

Seaweed-and-Miso

Cured Fish

Makes 1 to 11/2 pounds fish

I make this recipe, and riffs on it, as often as I can. It's a flavor powerhouse and produces an incredibly unique end result—a fish that is first cured to develop its flavor and then cooked. Use boneless or bone-in fish, steaks, or fillets.

Hell, you can go for it with a whole fish! I like sablefish, cod, salmon, halibut, and mackerel, but any fish will work great, both fresh- and saltwater. Scale up the ingredient amounts for larger amounts of fish.

1/2 cup	white miso
2 Tbsps.	mirin
1 tsp.	soy sauce (I used shoyu)
4 Tbsps.	sake or white wine
1 tsp.	Brad's Furikake (page 192) or store-bought furikake
1 to 1 1/2 pounds	fish (fillets, steaks, or whole fish)
1 to 2	large sheets dried or fresh kelp

In a small bowl, whisk together the miso, mirin, soy sauce, 1 tablespoon of the sake, and furikake. Rub the mixture all over the fish. Really get it on there. If using dried kelp, take a lint-free cloth or a fancy paper towel and dampen the towel and kelp with the remaining 3 tablespoons sake. If using fresh kelp, it will already be wet, so just pat it dry and use the sake to soak just the towel.

Wrap the fish with the seaweed to cover it all up like a nice little gift. Then wrap that with the damp cloth. Now place that all in a zip-close bag and refrigerate for 3 days. Yes, 3 days, but you can do just 2 if you want.

Continues on next page

Continued
from previous
page

Larger cuts of fish can and want to cure for longer than small, thin cuts do.

Unwrap the fish and scrape off the paste. (Or you can leave some on for added flavor.) You can fool around with different cooking methods at this point. I love to broil the cured fish in a preheated cast-iron pan in the oven. Grilling won't do you wrong either. The cure and magic between the ingredients is the takeaway. I just recommend cooking each type of fish as you'd prefer to cook that specific variety without this cure. Fatty fish that can take a good hammering of heat have given me great results.

The fish will pick up color from the cure depending on the miso you use. It will also add some sweetness, causing the fish to caramelize faster than usual, so keep in mind that it can burn. Hot-hot isn't always best, but sometimes it is…Enjoy!

Kelp-and-Mushroom Dashi

Makes 1 quart

Dashi is a family of Japanese broths made by steeping flavorful ingredients in water. It's a fantastic liquid base for all kinds of dishes. There are many types of dashi and regional variations; this is a version I love and use often in dishes like miso soup, but it's very versatile. Use it in place of water or other liquids in rice or soup or in braises to add a layer of umami-rich flavor—anywhere a lightly salted flavorful liquid could be replaced to be made better. I use one of two methods when I make dashi—one long and one short.

Continues on next page

Continued
from previous
page

1,000 grams (1 liter)	water
40 grams	dried kelp
15 grams	dried shiitake mushrooms
3 grams	bonito flakes

Short method: Heat everything except the bonito flakes together in a medium pot over medium heat until the temperature reaches about 150°F. Remove the pan from the heat and let steep for 20 minutes. Add the bonito flakes and continue to steep for 10 minutes longer.

Long method: Add everything but the bonito flakes to a jar or pot and let it steep at room temperature. I like to do a large batch in a glass sun-tea jar that I have. I place it in the sun all day and let it cool overnight before straining it. About an hour before I strain, I add the bonito flakes.

Either way, strain and use the dashi, or refrigerate for a few days or freeze for a few months. I consume it both hot and cold.

Flies and Sails

There's a definite theme to my travels, and you may notice that I love the water. I've never lived too far from the ocean. I need it, and as much as I love mountains and the middle of this country, I'm always drawn back to shorelines and waterways. I grew up fishing, but with a classic spinning rod. It wasn't until a couple years ago that I was introduced to the art of fly fishing. The sport is as much poetry to me as it is the pursuit of fish. I've learned that there are two things you walk away from fly fishing with an appreciation of: patience and the beauty of fishing itself.

8

Perfect form

This chapter is all about fly fishing in Vermont, one of the most terrible places in the country. (I'm kidding—it's one of my favorite spots in the Northeast.) I've spent most of my time in Vermont in and around Burlington and Lake Champlain. You can't help but be awed by its untouched beauty. So, I headed up north at the end of summer to chase trout on the fly rod and also get out on a buddy's sailboat. My local guide for the fly fishing was Captain Tony. Tony is a badass local who knows his waters better than most; he also runs a commercial fishing operation in Alaska. The Captain is legit! I met him through a good buddy of mine, Matt, who helps run and operate Hotel Vermont in Burlington. If you're up that way check it out, and tell Matt I sent you. That'll be good for one free beer. (Sorry Matt, LOL).

It's September in Vermont and I don't know a better place to spend a few days running around trying to catch trout. This particular summer was dry and warm late into the fall, which is less than ideal for trout fishing, as trout thrive in cold, well oxygenated freshwater. Hot, dry weather leads to rivers and creeks getting low and fish resorting to survival mode; they stop eating and slow down till the rains and cooler weather arrive.

In the course of exploring the locations featured in this book, I learned over and over that you cannot plan everything, least of all the weather. Trout are very fickle and don't care about you getting the perfect photograph or being successful at catching any fish! We fished for three days...and we fished hard, throwing every trick and fly we had at those fish. I managed to catch a rather large smallmouth bass and a few little fallfish, but no trout. But, in hindsight, as much as I wish we caught some beautiful brookies or rainbow trout, I'd likely just have let them go, especially if it wasn't a farmed trout.

Did you know that many rivers and streams are often stocked with farm-raised trout, released into the waters by the state's parks or wildlife department for people to catch and enjoy? It's often a huge operation that assists in sustaining and supporting healthy populations. In a lot of areas, wild fish are required to be released. I highly recommend looking into the local regulations before you start filling a cooler up under a bridge. We are the shepherds of the land. Look into it and get informed!

I could continue to make excuses as to why Captain Tony and I didn't catch a single trout in three full days of fishing, but instead I'll tell you how much I love smoked trout, when I can get it. If you are lucky, you might live near a good co-op or fishmonger who can get you some nice farmed rainbow trout. This breed farms rather well and doesn't destroy the ecosystem in the process; it's relatively cheap and underutilized as an ingredient. In my opinion, smoked trout is a perfect food and, when prepared and served well, an absolute treat. Salty and sweet with fatty and clean tight meat. The skin is like a wrapping paper for the perfect gift bundle of fish.

We headed back to the house and set a few beautiful farmed rainbow trout from a local fishmonger up on the smoker. The plan was to ditch my soggy waders (yes, I fell and flooded them), get some food and drinks together, and go meet up with Matt on his classy little sailboat in Burlington.

What's great about the recipes in this chapter is that they all keep well, so you can do the work ahead of time. Everything can be made a day ahead—work smarter not harder. For our trip, I smoked a nice chunk of beef to chill and use as sandwich meat and made some other cold dishes that travel well. I don't ever want to be the guy who shows up on a special day like this with store-bought lunchmeat, a plastic cheese plate, or a soggy sub from some deli. Those can all be great picnic options, but there's something to be said about making your own stuff. As my dad says, "The food you serve to friends is a representation of how you feel about them." I don't know how true that is for others, but I find myself saying it under my breath pretty often.

We met up with Matt in the middle of the afternoon. Lake Champlain was stunning; she never fails to blow me away when I look across her wide reflective water and see the lush green mountains meeting the shore on the New York side. Adirondack Park is a beautiful and special place and happened to be the backdrop for that evening's picnic on the lake.

The weather, always uncooperative, was moody with rain systems blowing around in the distant sky. I love to watch a rain cloud dumping water in the distance. The millions of drops come together to look like a dense fog falling, brooding and ominous but somehow still comforting. Ultimately, the rain didn't dampen our evening. We took a dip (you kind of have to), ate, and drank fine wine. We even got a nice gust of wind to do some proper sailing.

I don't need more hobbies, but one day I would like to own a small sailboat like Matt's. It's an old way of doing things: raw, simple, and unforgiving. Sailing one forces you to live in the moment, act simply, and work in concert with nature. It seems simple to the eye, but is complex in technique and difficult at times—all things which I can relate to life and cooking.

A great example of how to flood your waders

Smoked trout, the perfect food

Smoked Trout

Makes 3 smoked trout

I think smoked trout is the perfect fish. It is one of my favorite foods and I hope you make it at home. I'm always eating it cold. It's 100 percent a fantastic snack. It's great as is right out of the fridge eaten with your fingers, in a dip, or presented with the finest of meat and cheese on a platter. What's nice about smoked fish is that the meat peels easily off the body and leaves most of the bones behind. But you've still got to eat with care. In the world of bony things, smoked trout is no shad, I'll tell you that.

3	whole trout, cleaned
1 cup	soy sauce (I used shoyu)
1/2 cup	Fermented Pepper Paste (page 100)
1/2 cup	Fermented Mushroom-Kombu Shoyu (page 248)
1/4 cup	maple syrup
3 Tbsps.	miso
2 Tbsps.	mirin
2 Tbsps.	Pepper Mix (page 285)
5	garlic cloves, crushed and peeled
3 sheets	dried kombu (kelp)
2 to 3	fresh or dried hot peppers, crushed

Start by getting the finest trout you can get your hands on.

Make the marinade: Combine the remaining ingredients in a medium bowl, making sure the miso dissolves into the liquid, and wait for the kelp to hydrate. After a minute or two, once the kelp loses its dry, crunchy, brittleness and returns to its raw natural state, stuff it into the cavities of the fish. (I've also been known to take a fine needle and prick holes into the skin of the fish to allow more marinade to enter.) As with most recipes in this book, you can riff on the ingredients and flavor profiles here, but do be careful of salt and sugar amounts.

Place the fish and all the marinade into a snug vessel or zip-top bag so that the fish is covered in liquid. Refrigerate for 24 to 48 hours, depending on how much flavor you want pulled into the meat. Flip the fish about every 12 hours.

A note on smoking: You will need a rig of your choice or a smoking unit that can maintain a relatively steady temperature. I've seen people smoke trout successfully in all types of rigs ranging from modified metal filing cabinets to old Weber grills. The best advice is to run the machine a couple times first with a cheap piece of food (or even empty) to get familiar with how to control heat and smoke. The last thing you want to do is mess up the trout you've been marinating for a day or two. I like to run my smoker for trout on the low and slow side, keeping a temperature of about 145 to 160°F. Typically I burn applewood or cherrywood.

Remove the fish from the marinade and let them air dry on a rack set over a sheet pan in the fridge for an hour. I reserve about a cup of marinade to brush the skin of the fish once or twice during smoking. It gives the fish a nice color if nothing else, but it's not mandatory for a great result.

Preheat the smoker to 145 to 160°F, place the fish in the smoker, and smoke for 6 to 8 hours, or longer if you like your fish on the drier side. (Sometimes I like it smoked for just 5 hours, and sometimes I let it ride in the smoke for up to 12 hours to really dry out.) Keep an eye on the temperature gauge and on the fish; hotter-running units will result in a faster cook time. I'm sure you will taste a little piece right out of the smoker, but try to wait. I personally feel smoked trout really sings the next day when you take it out of the fridge.

The trout skin will peel back like paper, revealing perfect flesh underneath. The meat should peel right off the skeleton as a top loin and bottom belly meat. The trout keeps in the fridge for a week, but it never seems to make it that long.

Sunrise in Vermont

Cold
Root
Salad

Serves 6

This sounds like something my grandmother invented, and she probably did. No matter what party you go to, if you bring a cold root salad on a summer day, the platter will always end up empty. This is always a crowd pleaser, relatively cheap, and great to make a day ahead.

2 bunches	golden beets or a mix of beets and turnips
1 pound	baby Yukon Gold potatoes

Dressing

1/4 cup	extra-virgin olive oil
2 Tbsps.	lemon juice
1 Tbsp.	honey
2 tsps.	Brad's Furikake (page 192) or store-bought furikake
	kosher salt, to taste
	Pepper Mix (page 285), to taste
6 ounces	feta, crumbled or slabbed

I cook the root veggies both with and without the skin, it's a personal preference. But if you leave the skins on I do recommend scrubbing and rinsing them well before cooking.

Roast, steam, or boil the beets (and/or turnips) and potatoes until they're tender but not falling apart and mushy; the tip of a knife should pass into the veggies with ease. Once cooked, chill the roots in the fridge; this can be done up to two days ahead of time if you like.

In a small bowl or pint container, mix or whisk all the dressing ingredients together. When ready to eat, toss the root veggies and feta with the dressing and serve cold or at room temp.

Harvesting sumac

Sumac "Lemonade"

Makes 1 quart

This riff on sun tea is made with a sumac cone or cluster, honey, herbs, and lemon, and is scalable for large-batch brews.

Try to get the juiciest, freshest sumac berries you can find in a cluster the size of your forearm.

So how do you find it? Staghorn sumac is native to North America. Many people consider it a weed. I've noticed that the best place to find it is on the side of the road. It's that tropical-looking plant that many in the Northeast have seen but never thought much about. When the leaves go red later in the fall, that's when you want to go pick your staghorns.

For this beverage, a fresh sumac cluster is the best; don't mess around with using dried stuff because there's such a big gap between what you can get at the store and what you might find outside on your own. If you're out foraging for sumac, bring a little ladder or a pruner with you to reach high branches, like you're picking apples. And wear long sleeves, because the areas where sumac grows wild is primo real estate for poison ivy. You might think you'll be making sumac lemonade and end up getting shots in the hospital.

1	large staghorn **sumac** cluster
4 cups	**water**
3 Tbsps.	**honey** or maple syrup (optional)
1 sprig	fresh **mint** or tarragon
1	lemon, sliced, for garnish

Mix the **sumac, water, honey,** and **mint** together in a large glass vessel, cover, and let it steep in the sun as you would a sun tea, about 4 hours. My mom always did this with black and green tea, or just fresh herbs, and I remember loving it!

Strain. Store in the fridge. This beverage is so refreshing and cooling over ice with a lemon garnish, it's perfect for the whole damn family! For us, a batch disappears the same day it's made.

Note that you can speed up this process by making a hot concentrate: Steep the ingredients on the stovetop in a little hot water. Strain and cut with more liquid of your choice. I prefer the old sun-tea technique for whatever reason!

Smoked Beef

Serves 8

This is what most deli counter roast beef wishes it was. In addition to sandwiches, this meat is also amazing to cube up and use in fried rice or stir fries. Perfectly tender, even when reheated and crisp! Or add some, sliced thin (and with some flaky salt), to a little meat-and-cheese plate. You're welcome.

A big hunk of beef like this is something you really want to salt in advance of cooking it. Salt, unlike pepper and garlic powder and cumin and sugar, does go through cell membranes and penetrates into the meat. I learned that from a food scientist named Rosemary Trout, who is awesome.

1 solid 4-pound	boneless strip roast or other roasting cut
	kosher salt, to taste
2 Tbsps.	Pepper Mix (page 285)
1 Tbsp.	freshly ground coffee
1 Tbsp.	onion powder
1 Tbsp.	garlic powder
1 Tbsp.	sugar
1 tsp.	cocoa powder
1/2 tsp.	cayenne (optional for heat)
2 Tbsps.	extra-virgin olive oil

Rub the meat with as much salt as will stick to it, wrap in plastic, and refrigerate for 24 to 48 hours.

When ready to smoke, mix all the remaining ingredients except the olive oil together in a bowl. Pat the meat dry, rub with the olive oil, and then all over with the spice mixture.

Preheat a smoker or oven to 230°F. Place the meat in the smoker or in a roasting pan in the oven and bake for 2 hours, or until

Continues on next page

Continued
from previous
page

the center reaches 125°F. (This number is subject to change…You can lower it to 115°F if you're one of the folks who likes beef very pink, or raise it to 140°F if you're a well-doner.)

After it reaches the desired temperature, you're going to want to blast the meat at 500°F to finish it: First remove the meat from the oven or smoker and turn the heat up. Once it comes to temperature, place the meat back in and let it blast…but don't go too far away. It shouldn't take more than just a few minutes to get the outside to crisp and caramelize a bit.

Let the meat rest for at least 30 minutes, then wrap it in plastic and place in the fridge. I always eat some just after it has rested—how could I not? But this roast is meant for sandwiches! Slice as thick as you'd like (I'm a thin kind of guy). A little bit of mayo, salt and pepper, and tomatoes on fresh-baked sourdough (page 153) is what I love to enjoy on one of my favorite lakes!

Chickpea
Labneh

Makes a little more than 3 cups

Labneh is a Middle Eastern yogurt product that is drained through cheesecloth until it is almost the thickness of cream cheese. I like to mix it with chickpeas and almonds, which give it a nice viscosity and a nutty flavor that rounds it out, adding depth and body and making the labneh more filling. It's no longer a dip, it's more of a side.

2 cups	full-fat yogurt (not Greek)
1/2 cup	chickpeas, drained and mashed
2 Tbsps.	raw almonds, toasted
2 Tbsps.	Marcona almonds kosher salt, to taste
3 Tbsps.	honey
2 Tbsps.	lemon juice
3	sprigs fresh mint extra-virgin olive oil thin slices sourdough bread, toasted hard, or crackers, for dipping

In a small mixing bowl, combine the yogurt, chickpeas, raw almonds, and Marcona almonds and mix well. Scrape all into a large piece of cheesecloth and twist into a ball, causing the whey (liquid) to start to seep out. Don't force it.

Tie the cheesecloth closed with a long piece of string and set it up so it hangs over a bowl to drain. Get creative if you need to. Drain the yogurt in the fridge overnight, or until the texture is as thick as you want.

Sometimes I hang it for an hour or two, and sometimes for 2 days. Longer will make it drier, so it's up to you.

Fold the honey and lemon juice into the labneh. Drizzle with olive oil and serve with the mint alongside bread or crackers for dipping.

Marinated

Serves 4

Something magical happens when you cook beans from scratch and serve with a vinaigrette-like sauce. Go ahead, throw some mushrooms in there.

Beans

1 pound	dried beans (your favorite)
2 sheets	dried kombu (kelp)

Vinaigrette

1/2 cup	extra-virgin olive oil
1/4 cup	champagne vinegar
1 Tbsp.	honey
1 Tbsp.	Dijon mustard
1/4 cup	toasted hazelnuts, chopped
1 head	roasted garlic (see page 336)
1/4 cup	fresh chives and any other mixed herbs in your life
1 Tbsp.	fresh thyme leaves

Rinse the dried beans and pick through them to remove any debris. Place in a large or medium-large pot and cover with 6 inches of cold water. Bring to a hard simmer, then reduce the heat to medium low. Add the kombu and simmer the beans until tender but not falling apart. Timing will depend on the type of bean. Drain the beans and place in a bowl or vessel of choice.

For the vinaigrette: Whisk all the ingredients together. Pour over the beans while still hot and fold together until coated. I eat them at room temperature if I'm going to finish them that day. Or, store in the fridge and pull them out for a side dish with all your meals.

Brad's Za'atar

Makes about 1 cup

Za'atar is a popular spice mix that exists in variations all over the Middle East, and now the world. Not only do versions vary from region to region, but family recipes vary from house to house as well. I love that, so here's mine—even though I did not grow up with the spice mix, and my parents may still not know how to pronounce za'atar or even what it is. But I find myself putting it in everything. It brings a brightness that can be surprising—that's the sumac—and that is perfect alongside the dried herbs and sesame seeds. It marries well with almost any savory profile.

I toast my sesame and coriander seeds in the oven until they become nutty and fragrant. I do this using separate baking sheets since they toast at different rates. Grinding your own coriander for this makes for a highly aromatic blend.

1/2 cup	dried oregano
1/2 cup	dried thyme
1/2 cup	dried marjoram
1/4 cup	ground sumac
5 Tbsp.	toasted sesame seeds
1 tsp.	toasted coriander seed, ground
1 tsp.	extra-virgin olive oil
1 Tbsp.	kosher salt (optional)

Mix **all the ingredients** together in a medium bowl. Store in an airtight container for up to a few weeks. Sprinkle it on everything!

Some folks will sneeze just looking at this photo.

9

Fascinating Fungus

Butter-sauteed chicken of the woods, one of my favorite mushroom preparations

Here's a fun little fact: Fungus is actually more similar in its DNA structure to humans than it is to plants. I've been slightly obsessed with fungus my whole life, and the more I learn, the more I realize I'm just getting started. There are people who've dedicated their lives to learning about fungus and mycelium, which refers to the vegetative part of mushrooms that you don't see: the fine network of filaments growing below the ground.

Mushrooms are so much more than sliced creminis on your pizza. Fungi are actually one of the most important and unique life-forms on the planet, key players in the symbiotic relationships that support all life and food systems. Going back to high school science class, mushrooms are both consumers and decomposers. This means that mushrooms are able to consume and then break down (decompose) decaying organisms on the forest floor. They put life back into the Earth, and they're damn good at it.

If this sounds interesting to you, look up one of the many writers and scientists researching this stuff. One of my favorites is Paul Stamets, whose work first sent me down this fascinating rabbit hole. He spoke about a section of forest in western Washington State, the Hoh Rainforest, which is this country's largest temperate rainforest. It's insanely beautiful and home to the largest network of underground mycelium. This blew me away. For the longest time I had only paid attention to the visible flowering/reproductive parts of fungus. (My wife might argue that I'm not much different toward her. Sorry, bad joke.) But like my wife, there is so much more to mushrooms than an intriguing and unique exterior; there are complex systems at play, making major contributions to our world. That strange-looking mushroom growing on a shady log after a rainstorm is so much more than a potential snack.

Some of the first wild mushrooms that I fell in love with were chanterelles, maitakes, and morels. All are delicious, along with being pretty easy to identify and usually found right in your neighbor's yard or the woods of the Northeast. My old man had a spot by a big oak tree where we'd find a little cornucopia of perfect mushrooms while out bow hunting. One perk to hunting in the woods is that you are always able to scout for mushrooms or other wild edibles. I get excited thinking about the next time I stumble upon a new patch.

Once you find your own spot, you have a little secret that's yours to manage and protect. It becomes your baby. To me it's like having the best little farmers' market all to yourself—truly magical. But as delicious as mushrooms are, they can be equally hard to find. Hidden under pine needles or fallen leaves or the lush forest floor, mushrooms are masters of camouflage. I've got some buddies who take their kids with them foraging, and I'm jealous of how many mushrooms they find together. Fresh, curious eyes that are a shorter distance to the ground are always helpful in foraging.

I'm convinced that we've passed by or walked over countless mushrooms—even the boldly colored chanterelle, which can be bright yellow and orange. But when I do see them, it flushes me with a sense of accomplishment. Like field mice in the walls, where there's one there must be more, so watch your step once you score.

Remember, you want to harvest just the flower. The mushroom actually lives in the soil beneath the surface, so be careful when harvesting to avoid tearing up the ground and the fragile mycelium network beneath it. Get a sharp little knife—you can call it your "mushroom foraging knife"—and keep it in a little sheath. Take this with you when you're out there, and use it to simply cut the base of the stem near the soil, nice and clean. Put your prize in a basket, leaving the complex root system undisturbed in the ground. Then, get back to looking for more edible beauties.

I've heard from experts that wicker baskets are best to carry the mushrooms while foraging because they allow the mushrooms to drop spores while you walk. I almost don't want to fact-check that, but it sure as hell sounds like a good idea to me. Even if a basket is not an effective spore-spreader, it's still a great way to transport mushrooms. It's reusable and allows for air circulation, which is crucial in maintaining your harvest's freshness.

Mushrooms need to breathe, so putting them in something silly like a plastic bag will cause them to moisten and spoil quickly. Don't spend your day walking in the woods finding the best mushrooms only to render them unusable due to poor handling. I've been there, I'll sadly admit. I once was in a pinch and had nothing but a plastic shopping bag to use. It wouldn't be the end of the world if you left it open for a couple hours, but it didn't work out for me that day.

As delicious and fun as all this sounds, there are serious dangers that can come with picking wild mushrooms. The wrong mushrooms can leave you very ill and can even result in organ failure or death. It is

Mycelium being grown

234

absolutely no joke. Please do not go winging it in the woods. I'm thirty-five years old and only just became comfortable enough to pick and eat wild mushrooms by myself. I say "by myself" because I didn't start out that way. No one should. Hell, I still prefer having an expert with me when foraging.

Fungus Friends are good friends to have, and I worked with a few in the course of writing this book. They are folks who have put the work in to become true experts. You want to learn from someone who gets super excited when you find a fat patch and easily identifies the mushrooms by their Latin names—they are equally interested in the mushrooms you grill as they are in the ones that cause liver failure. My buddies James and Evan are my Fungus Friends and every time I go out with them I learn more. If you're lucky

enough to find friends like them, treat them right. They might let you in on some secret world-class locations.

Mushroom foraging, like fishing, leads its enthusiasts to lament about missed opportunities and boast about the best days, the typical "Oh man, you guys should've been here last week" kind of situation. We found lots of mushrooms this year, but only because we kept looking all over the Northeast, from Jersey to Maine, every chance we had. Making a mushroom chapter was actually pretty difficult because the Northeast experienced one of the driest summers in recorded history. Dry forests are not ideal for mushrooms, which tend to pop up when their environment is consistently moist.

Species like morels and chanterelles eluded us, but James led us to some cool

Farmed mushrooms

spots for button mushrooms, maitakes, and a few other species that I had never heard of. Earlier in the year, while we were up in Maine cooking seaweed and shellfish for the Vacationland chapter with my friend Evan, he showed up with two massive baskets of gorgeous chanterelles and black trumpets. They were perfect in every way. But amid the hustle and bustle and other distractions, we missed out on those beauties. I still feel bad about it.

Anyway, my Fungus Friends and I packed up the gear and drove to meet another friend with a little operation where logs are inoculated with fungus spores and left to grow naturally. He harvested mushrooms like oyster and shiitakes on a schedule that could be managed pretty easily—an awesome little hobby. He told us he had a massive wild hen-of-the-woods spot in perfect condition, growing in his yard by an old oak stump. He'd been protecting it with a little fence and watering it through the dry months. We arrived and realized we found our white whale! It was such a perfect cluster we almost didn't want to pick it...almost. It would actually have been a shame not to pick those babies at their prime, because in a few days they would have begun to rot and break down. HOME RUN!

We visited one more Fungus Friend who runs a fantastic (and creative) mushroom farming operation out of modified shipping containers. He turns the units into perfectly controlled, ideal microclimates, allowing mushrooms to flourish. As we walked into the units, it looked like a sci-fi movie. There were flowering fungi of all colors, looking like something from another planet through the dim lighting and eerie mist from the watering system. My eyes widened as I saw some of my favorites—oysters, trumpets, hen-of-the-woods, and lion's mane. I bought a box of them to play with back at the fire pit, and later I saved the stems and scraps to dehydrate and restock my home supply.

Cooking with mushrooms is straightforward. Many vegetarians use mushrooms as a meat alternative because they tend to have firm textures and take so well to such a variety of cooking methods and seasonings. They are the ultimate product of their environments, earthy and robust in flavor or super mild and delicate. One mushroom of the same species can taste totally different depending on its growing conditions. I get just as fired up about cultivated mushrooms as I do the wild ones. Whatever the source, add some salt and fat over high heat, and finish them with a little acid, and you're in good shape. Note that with many wild mushrooms, it's recommended to cook them rather than eating them raw.

Just like rock climbing, hiking, and fishing, mushroom foraging has a large community of people who are usually more than happy to share their passion and welcome you into the woods. If you're lucky enough to meet some Fungus Friends, go for a walk with them. Even if you don't pick or eat anything, you'll learn so much and have some fun being in the woods with good people. You'll also see the forest with fresh eyes and newfound respect for nature. Be a good person, play by the rules, and maybe you'll find yourself a Fungus Friend. When you do, hold on tight, because they're the best friends to have.

Dried
Mushrooms

Makes as much as you have

Most mushrooms are best prepped and eaten right away and my favorite methods of cooking are usually very simple. But if you have an abundance of mushrooms or any leftover scraps, try drying them instead of discarding them. This is easily done in a few ways:

1. Naturally dry them, spaced out in a warm, dry place.

2. Thread them together (with cooking string) and hang them in a well-circulated area.

3. Bake them at very low temperature (like 150°F for about an hour) spaced on a parchment-lined baking sheet.

4. Use a dehydrator, low and slow.

My mom would hang them from the wire rack in the laundry room and check on them every once in a while. Whatever method you use, they're done when they are dry and crisp. Store them in an airtight container.

After they have dried, you can then powder the mushrooms in a blender, making for easy storage and interesting recipes. Try folding powdered mushrooms into flatbread dough or toss it into a braise or stock. Just like our ocean friend sugar kelp, dried powdered mushrooms are a fantastic way to boost umami and depth of flavor in any recipe. Keep a jar in your spice cabinet and you'll be surprised how often you reach for it.

Maitake (hen of the woods)

Grilled
Maitakes

Pressed and grilled maitake clusters, dressed with olive oil and vinegar, are a contender for any main dish. This is not just something that goes with a more familiar main protein as a side— these mushrooms will compete with any steak, chicken, or fish.

Whether farmed or wild, maitakes have so much flavor going on. They're easy to cook and can take a crisping— in fact, they almost need a hard sear. Like anything that comes from the wild, they have lots of subtle nuance in flavor depending on where they were harvested.

1 pound	maitake (hen-of-the-woods) mushroom clusters, either in a large single cluster or a bunch of smaller clusters
1/4 cup plus 2 Tbsps.	extra-virgin olive oil, plus more for coating the mushrooms
2 Tbsps.	rice vinegar
2 tsps.	honey
1 tsp.	ground sumac
3 Tbsps.	chopped fresh chives

Whisking a little miso into the vinaigrette will give the dressing a beautiful umami component.

Drizzle the mushrooms with a little olive oil and grill over medium-high heat or cook in a skillet on the stovetop. (Cooking mushrooms over a hardwood fire is never a bad idea as the smoky, woody flavor matches nicely with their earthy qualities and tangy dressing.) Cook until the small bits are crispy but the mushrooms remain tender and juicy inside.

To make the dressing, whisk the vinegar, honey, and sumac together before slowly whisking in the olive oil. Once a nice emulsification forms, fold in the chives. (The dressing can be made a day ahead, but if you do that, hold off on adding the chives until right before serving.) Drizzle the dressing over the grilled mushrooms and serve hot or at room temperature.

Chant and Plant

Dip

This mixture of chanterelles and eggplants (either hot or cold) is good on sandwiches, as a condiment for any meal, or just for dipping warm bread into. Eggplants and mushrooms may seem like unusual flavors to pair together, but to me they have a lot more in common than we give them credit for. They're both made of spongy, fibrous matter, and when you marry them together with olive oil, it's a trifecta made in heaven—grassy, earthy, vegetal. The eggplants fall apart, and the mushrooms become tender.

1 pound	eggplant, peeled and diced
8 ounces	chanterelles or mixed mushrooms
1 cup (or more)	extra-virgin olive oil
3	garlic cloves, chopped
1	dried chile (optional for heat)
1	fresh herb sprig (optional)
	kosher salt, to taste

Place the eggplant and mushrooms in a deep saucepan and cover with olive oil. The size of the pan will be a factor in the amount of oil you need. It's okay if the eggplant is not totally submerged, as it will release a lot of moisture and deflate as it cooks. Add the garlic to the pan, along with the chile and herb sprig if using.

Bring the oil to a bubbling simmer over medium-high heat. Simmer for about 5 minutes before reducing the temperature to low and allowing the eggplant to cook until it falls apart, about half an hour longer. Discard the chile and herb sprig. Season to taste with salt and serve hot or cold. The dip will keep refrigerated for a week.

Fermented Mushroom-Kombu Shoyu

Makes about 12 ounces

This is a fun and easy two-for-the-price-of-one recipe. You're welcome. I store the fermented shiitakes and the nutty, intensely flavorful shoyu together in the fridge, pulling mushrooms out as I need them, and drawing off the shoyu as I want. The flavor of the shoyu changes over time. It gets aggressive, then mellows, then gets real nutty. You'll find yourself grabbing it and using it all the time. It's good with anything that you want to add depth and salt to. I thinly slice the shiitake caps and use anywhere I would like a mushroom.

12 ounces	shoyu (your favorite bottle, such as Moromi)
8 ounces	fresh shiitake mushrooms, stems removed
1 sheet	dried kombu (kelp)
2 Tbsps.	mirin
1 Tbsp.	rice vinegar

Place all ingredients in a quart jar and cover the top with a piece of cloth secured with a rubber band. Allow to ferment for about 1 week at room temperature, out of the sun.

After a week, the mushrooms should be saturated and dense with a tender texture, having absorbed some of the shoyu and wilted a little. Cover with a lid and refrigerate for up to several months.

I've been known to dehydrate the kombu after the ferment and use it again in different applications, but I take no responsibility for this experiment.

Steak and Shrooms with Saucy Sauce

With access to great mushrooms and great steak, I had to bring back the old steakhouse classic: mushrooms and steak with sherry and butter. There's no reinvention here. I just want to teach you how to cook a good steak. (Here's how: Sear all the sides and rest it.)

1	bone-in New York strip steak, 1 1/2 to 2 inches thick
	kosher salt
2 Tbsps.	extra-virgin olive oil
1 pound	mixed wild mushrooms, halved if large

Saucy Sauce

3	garlic cloves, crushed and peeled
4 Tbsps.	salted butter
1/2 cup	sherry
1 to 2 sprigs	fresh aromatic herbs
	kosher salt and Pepper Mix (page 285), to taste

A day ahead, sprinkle the steak with salt and refrigerate.

Heat a large skillet or cast-iron pan over medium-high heat. There's nothing wrong with placing a cast-iron on the grill or on an outdoor burner; cooking steaks inside is fine, and it may be necessary for some, but it can leave the kitchen smoky.

Rub the meat with 1 tablespoon of the oil and place it fat-cap down in the pan. I like to cook the fat cap first to render out some of that fat to help cook the mushrooms.

Continues on next page

Continued
from previous
page

Add the mushrooms and remaining oil around the meat to begin the browning process. After the fat cap is seared and the fat has rendered, place the steak on the bone end and cook for a few minutes; heating the bone will transmit the heat through the meat and help it cook evenly, rather than having the bone shield some of the meat.

Stir the mushrooms when needed, then place the steak flat-side down to begin searing all the sides. Every steak will cook differently, so I don't want to give exact times here. Watch your steak. Touch your steak. Observe the changes and use your intuition and gut to guide you. You're a better cook than you think. It's just a steak and mushrooms.

When the steak reaches your desired temp, let it rest on a wire rack. (Leave the mushrooms in the pan.) I pull mine at 130°F and let it rest for 30 minutes, although steak can rest up to an hour before serving.

For the sauce: I slice my steak and have it ready to serve right before I build this pan sauce. Add the garlic and butter to the mushrooms in the pan and allow the butter to melt over medium-high heat. Once the butter is nice and bubbly, add the sherry and herbs and simmer hard for a couple minutes until the liquid thickens nicely—just a few minutes, and I like to stir rapidly. Spoon the buttery mushroom sauce over the sliced meat and season with a little salt and fresh pepper mix.

Whatever

Waters off Stonington, Connecticut, Mid–Autumn

Fish

10

Growing up, I fished a lot at local lakes with my friends. At around ten years old, we were given the freedom to ride our bikes to the lakes surrounding our neighborhoods, and we did that all summer long. My mom threw "fishing birthday parties" for me, carting food, snacks, and a cake down to the lake. Friends brought their poles and we'd cast and catch together for a few hours. As we got older, we chained small metal jon boats to a tree near the lake. Those boats opened up opportunity: We could get out to spots we could never cast to from shore. After all, that's where all the friggin' fish are!

My dad was the one who introduced me to a rod and reel and spent time with me at these lakes, but his true love is saltwater fishing. My sister and I often went out with him on the ocean. We lived a few hours from the beach, so any saltwater expedition required getting up at 4:30 a.m. for the drive. A few of Dad's friends had their own boats, but most often we'd pay to go on a public party boat or a private charter. Either way, once you're out there, catching a fish is not guaranteed. We came home empty-handed pretty frequently, having failed to catch a single fish (or one that met the requirements to keep). As a young kid, that sucked.

Looking back now, I know that money was tight and it must have been a big deal for my dad to save up for those trips. Those days were important to him and he wanted to spend them with us. I wish I hadn't gotten bored so easily, and that I had appreciated more of the joy and beauty of being on the water together. But that's how it is as we get older. Hindsight is 20/20.

Successful saltwater fishing requires a few skills and some good gear and knowledge, and having a solid group of friends and guides adds to the fun. Even the most hardened fishermen will tell stories of the old-timer who taught him to rig a jig that the fatties can't refuse. Being with the right folks to show you the good spots can make all the difference, and navigating the water is just as important as knowing how to catch the fish, if not more so. Things can turn from fun to a nightmare if you don't know how to manage your vessel.

On the ocean, things go from being slow to fast-paced and intense in the blink of an eye. Once you feel that nibble, that little tug on the line, it's time to get moving. A good fish will start running your line *fast* and there will be an explosive zzzzzzzzzzzz on the reel. The trip from boring to pure adrenaline takes a split second.

Geologically speaking, the continental shelf extends from land, hits the ocean, and maintains relatively consistent water depth for miles heading out into the Atlantic. Much farther offshore, there are canyons, gulf streams, and vast open waters for deep-sea fishing. But for this chapter, we stayed relatively close in where many of my favorite fish live, fishing in the waters between Montauk, New York; Mystic, Connecticut; and Cape Cod, Massachusetts. These cold, fertile waters make for some of the best saltwater fishing on the planet, and are best known for big, glorious striped bass.

I love getting into the big, fat, hog-like bass that are the size of Shaq's leg. But there's much more out there to catch. Keep in mind the conservation of the species: Because everyone wants to catch and eat bass, their population numbers have to be closely monitored. I'm skating on a complex topic here, but we can't only catch and eat the most popular fish. Chasing smaller and less "favorable" species can be just as fun and tasty, and takes pressure off overfished species. In a time when the ocean and its inhabitants are struggling, this is the least we can do.

Baitfish travel in what looks like a huge ball moving through the water. These dark spots are densely packed schools swimming tightly together, cruising the shallows. Swimming in schools is a defense mechanism that evolved as protection from

World-class
black sea bass

predators and for improved foraging. It requires coordinated body positions and synchronized movement, which is pretty impressive for these little guys. And where they go, larger fish follow.

Enter the bluefish, a no-nonsense fish that fears nothing and is eager to bite almost anything you throw at it. Armed with a nasty set of teeth and meat that has been described as too oily to eat, fishermen in the old days regarded it as a junk fish. But done right, blues are some of my favorite fish to catch and eat. Other lesser-known fish like flats, shad, black sea bass, bonita, sea robins, and dogfish cruise these waters too. Not all are popular to catch, but my dad always told me you can eat anything that comes from the ocean. This has rung true so far!

What makes a junk fish? Ultimately,

My dad and Vinny catching shad

A sea robin

258

it's less about the fish itself and more about how you handle and treat your catch. Some fish require a little more respect and delicate care to ensure that the meat inside is preserved. For example, if you catch a bluefish, hit it on the head, and let it flop around on the deck in stress for 30 minutes, you can bet that fish is not going to be a great eating experience. But it doesn't have to be that way. Letting a fish suffer degrades its flavor—not to mention that it's just mean.

I don't care if it's a porgy, weakfish, bass, or tuna, when you catch a fish, treat it right. As soon as it's on deck, kill the fish as quickly as possible (almost instantly) by shocking its brain and central nervous system with a spike. *Ikejime* is the Japanese name for this process. Killing the fish quickly prevents a bad scene: The life of the fish is respected and your dinner tastes better. Don't make it a junk fish by disregarding a safe and respectful method of harvest. And if you're not planning to eat the fish you caught, throw it back while it's alive.

Once the fish is dead, bleed it out. I do this within a minute of the fish leaving the water. Use a sharp knife or snips to cut the main gill arteries, then gently massage the fish from tail to head. This causes most of the blood to pump out of the cut gill quickly. Blood left in the meat is what usually makes fish taste and smell bad or "fishy." After the fish is cleaned and bled out, pack it onto ice...and that fish is set. Sushi grade!

Generally, I avoid filleting fish. I prefer to cook them whole or cut into steaks because cooking on the bones adds so much flavor and helps retain moisture. You can grill, fry, or roast a whole fish as well. Don't worry much about the bones; once cooked the meat tends to fall right off. Most of the time, if fish are treated properly when caught, they don't really need much and can go with just about anything. Apply any spice profile you desire from spicy to sweet to both at once. If you kill and process a 3-pound bluefish properly, pack it on ice, and grill it whole with some salt, butter, and garlic, it'll be juicy and white in color and have so much flavor.

If you do fillet a fish, keep the bones and the head to make stock. Add some herbs, leeks, garlic, spices, and water and let it simmer, and you'll create a rich and nourishing liquid that sets up like jelly when cooled. Now you've got another little secret flavor weapon.

The fishing trips we went on for this chapter were all top-notch days on the water. Nothing but laughter and home runs, by which I mean catching fish on every cast. We were inshore, never out of land's sight, and sometimes right on the beach. To decide where to go, we searched the horizon to find birds flocking to feed on small fish erupting from the water. It literally looked like water exploding, with so many small baitfish jumping to avoid capture by larger fish that the birds then noticed and got in on the action. They circled above as the big fish feasted on the smaller baitfish, then dove to pick up whatever they could.

I call this spectacle a "mad blitz" and it's a surefire sign of where you should cast a line. Get there fast and you're bound to catch something. I've even seen where the fish roll right up onto the beach chasing the bait. As you pull those bass and blues out of the water, they'll spit dozens of smaller "whatevers" out of their mouths. (I define "whatevers" as whatever smaller fish or squid are being eaten at the time—undetermined and unidentified.)

Later on, we got into shad and bass schools so thick and dense, they seemed fake. It was like a dream come true: If your lure happened to reach the bottom, you came up with a legal-size black sea bass. Unbelievable. Fishing days like this are what folks dream of.

If this had been one of my first times out, it might have probably ruined fishing for me in the future—especially knowing the hours I've spent not catching a single fish, or adding up all the times I've been seasick. But I can't help but feel total appreciation for the opportunity to catch, handle, and cook fish like this.

My goal with this story is to share my love of going out to catch and cook quality fish. Try eating something that isn't tuna or salmon; and if you can, go drop a line in the water and handle a fish yourself. I promise it will change things for you. The connection and responsibility you'll feel when cooking and consuming that meat is truly a special experience.

What looks like rain hitting the water is actually thousands of fish exploding on a bait ball. I call it a "mad blitz."

Grilled Bone-In Fish

Serves 1 to 2

Fish cooked whole, in a pan or grilled (or cut in pieces and roasted over an open fire) might intimidate some. But the cooking is really quite simple. All you need is salt and oil, and if you don't want to make the spoon sauce, some herbs and citrus to serve with it. Bone-in is one of my favorite ways to cook fish, or any meat for that matter. The bones help the fish retain heat and hold in its juices, just like a bone-in steak.

1   whole fish
     extra-virgin olive oil
     kosher salt
     Spoon Sauce for Fish (next page), for serving

Heat a grill or pan to medium or medium high, depending on the size of your fish; the larger the fish, the lower the temp should be. You don't want the outside to burn before the inside cooks—thinking it looks great on the outside but then opening it up to find that the flesh is still raw. It does take some time and practice to figure out a good heat level where you get some char on the outside by the time the inside by the spine has just become juicy and starting to release from the bones. But don't go overboard, you're cooking fish, not chili. Just keep an eye on it.

Scale the fish and pat dry. (You can ask your fishmonger to scale a whole fish or cut it into steaks if you aren't comfortable doing that yourself.) Rub it with oil and salt, coating it inside and out. You can do all this a little ahead of time if you like.

Then put the fish on the grill or in the pan and let it cook. The scariest part is knowing

Continues on next page

Continued
from previous
page

when and how to flip or remove the fish. Do *not* try to flip the fish until it wants to release from the pan or grill. If it's sticking, just wait a little longer. You can also add a little bit of oil if the pan is looking dry. The worst thing to do is go scraping and ripping at it, resulting in one ugly torn-up fish. Use a fish spatula or a really flexible thin metal spatula; if you don't own one, it's time to make that investment. The fish will release when it's ready, but even now I still screw one up from time to time. If and when that happens, don't beat yourself up, the fish will still be delicious, you just won't get that classic picture we all love!

To fillet the fish after cooking, I use a fish spatula and a butter knife to separate the flesh of one side from the backbone. Then pull the spine out, and eat the bottom.

Spoon Sauce for Fish

Makes 2 1/2 cups

I like to make this a day ahead and add the herbs right before serving, as this will let the sauce get all saucy. Spoon it over grilled or roasted fish or use it as the base for a crudo or ceviche. The cherries add a little tart, sour brightness to it. A little seaweed powder might get thrown in, sometimes sesame seeds too...why not?

1 cup	extra-virgin olive oil
2 Tbsps.	white shoyu
1 cup	citrus segments, any mix (lime, grapefruit, use the best stuff you can find), diced
1/2 cup	mint, tarragon, and scallion greens
2 Tbsps.	grated fresh ginger
2 Tbsps.	dried cherries, chopped
1 Tbsp.	minced fresh chile pepper, or to taste (for optional heat)

Mix all the ingredients together in a bowl.
Taste and adjust how you like. This is just a
fun open canvas to use seasonal ingredients to
complement some great fish.

From catching it, to looking
at it, to eating it, bonito has
always been one of my favorites.

Crudo

4 to 6 servings

If you're in a place where you've got
great access to fresh fish, I've got you
covered with this crudo. Easy to make,
always a crowd-pleaser. I've never
made this for someone who didn't like
it. It's easy to adjust to different tastes
and comes together quickly.

8 ounces	sushi-grade fish fillet, such as sea bass, fluke, or any fish you can consume raw
1/4 cup	white shoyu
2 Tbsps.	pink grapefruit juice
2 Tbsps.	yuzu juice, fresh or bottled (see Note)
1 Tbsp.	navel orange juice
1 Tbsp.	lime juice
1 Tbsp.	finely grated fresh ginger
2 to 3 Tbsps.	nice extra-virgin olive oil
1/2 tsp.	powdered toasted nori
1/2 tsp.	powdered dried dulse
	kosher salt, for serving

Whether you bought or caught the fish, trim
any undesirable or tough bits from the fillet.
Keep your fish in a cold fridge or place it in the
freezer for a couple minutes to firm it up and
allow for easy slicing.

Start to slice the fish against the grain like
you would red meat. Using your sharpest and
longest knife, use the entire length of the blade
from the heel (closest part to the handle) to
the tip to *slice* the fish, not *chop* it. You want
clean cuts that keep the fish beautiful and
intact. How thin or thick you want to cut is a
personal preference and also depends on the
species. As you work, lay the slices out on a
pre-chilled platter; I like to leave a little space
between each piece.

Mix together the shoyu and all of the juices in
a small bowl. Mix in the ginger. You don't need

If you can't
find yuzu
juice, add an
additional 2
tablespoons
of one of the
other citrus
juices instead.

Continues on
next page

Continued
from previous
page

to use all the mixture if you don't want, but pour the juices around the sliced fish. Drizzle the best olive oil you can over the citrus and fish.

Blend the dried seaweeds on high in a spice grinder until they become a fine powder. I place the powder in a fine strainer and tap over the crudo platter, with a sprinkle of salt, to dust as a tasty and healthy garnish.

Eat right away, or let sit in the fridge for a few minutes to let the citrus juices work some magic with the fish. If you let it sit too long it's not a problem, the fish just becomes more of a ceviche than a crudo. Depending on the fish and my mood, I might do that on purpose!

Pickled Pickers

Makes 2 quarts

These are some nice pickled veggies that are fun to eat on their own or chop up and use as an ingredient in another dish. They're particularly good with fish, offering crunchy contrast and bright flavor. If I happen to have grilled a bunch of fish and have leftover fillets or chunks, the next day I'll take that fish, make some aioli, chop some of this up, and make myself a little fish salad. Or I'll mix them with mayonnaise and use in a cold grilled fish sandwich. If you like more heat, leave the seeds in the chile; if not, remove them or leave the chile out altogether.

You can also mix all of the vegetables together in a crock or jar, ditch the vinegar, and substitute more water until all the veg is covered. Put cheesecloth over the top, secured with a rubber band, and ferment at room temperature for a few days or up to a week. These lacto-fermented pickles will be a little funky and much less sharply acidic than a straight-up vinegar pickle.

1 pound	**mixed veggies** (carrots, cucumbers, cauliflower, radishes, mushrooms), cut into quarters or halves
	fresh chile, cut into thin strips (optional for heat)
1 cup	rice vinegar
1 cup	filtered water
2 Tbsps.	honey
1	garlic clove, thinly sliced
6	fresh bay leaves, crushed
1 Tbsp.	Pepper Mix (page 285)
1 tsp.	Brad's Za'atar (page 227) or store-bought
	kosher salt, equal to 2 percent of the total weight of all the above ingredients (liquids included) combined

Place **all the veggies** in jars or other vessels. I use crocks and bowls or jars, as long as the veg sits in liquid. Add the chile, if using.

Combine the remaining ingredients in a saucepan and warm on the stovetop. Don't let the liquid get hot, just warm…like the temperature you give a child a bath in, but maybe a little hotter. Stir until the salt dissolves. Add a little more vinegar or water to adjust to your taste.

Pour the liquid over the veggies. Let sit at room temperature for a couple hours before serving. Or place in the fridge and allow all the ingredients to get to know each other for a day or two. Eat the pickles with everything.

Serves 2 to 3

I love tinned fish like sardines and
mackerel, and this fresher version makes
a great snack or meal. I serve it with
rice or as taco filling when hot, and
as a sandwich or a salad topper when
cold. Or I'll put it on a board with some
Pickled Pickers (page 270) or other pickled
veggies dressed with a little oil and vinegar.
I've also been known to cook fish gently
in the oil until medium, remove it from
the oil, and blast it under a hot broiler to
quickly crisp up the skin, then serve hot.

Oil-Poached

Bone-In

Fish

2 cups	extra-virgin olive oil
3	garlic cloves, crushed and peeled
3	lemon zest strips
3	bay leaves
2 sprigs	fresh tarragon
1 tsp.	pink peppercorns, crushed
1 pound	fish steaks, salted a day ahead

Combine the oil, garlic, lemon zest, bay leaves, tarragon, and peppercorns in a medium pot and heat over medium heat to 150 to 170°F. Add the fish and gently poach until the meat starts to become opaque and feel firm yet tender. It might be 20 minutes, it might be an hour, depending on the thickness of the cut and the species used. It can certainly take longer with some big-boned fish. I like it closer to well-done if I'm planning to eat it cold, and medium-ish if eating it hot. It'll keep in the fridge for a day or two.

Delaware Water Gap

11

I grew up in Vernon, New Jersey, a rural town covering about 70 square miles with a population of roughly 22,000 people. There was only one stoplight in the center of town, and no fast food or convenience stores. Unless you're from there, you might not believe you're still in Jersey— you're nowhere near the Turnpike. We were surrounded by nature, and it was the kind of place where you ran around with your neighborhood pals all day long.

You could bum a lunch or snack at any house on the street and you could tell where everyone was by the bikes parked out front. There were no streetlights that went on at dusk. Instead, moms yelled down the street to call you home for dinner. The friends that I grew up with became my family. I'm so grateful for my childhood, as I'm not sure what I described really exists anymore. My parents still live in my childhood home and I go back to visit often.

I headed up there one weekend to visit and then went out to explore the Delaware Water Gap for this chapter. It took about 40 minutes to drive from my parents' house to a great spot on the Gap. Some of my favorite memories as a young man were swinging in and under waterfalls out on the border of Pennsylvania. I still bring new friends here and everyone is always in awe of the clear waterfalls, quiet woods, secluded privacy, and good old-fashioned swimming holes. It's an untouched slice of the Northeast. Granted, you need to know where to go, but it's less than 2 hours from Manhattan and a gem of the East Coast.

The Delaware Water Gap is basically the area around the Delaware River as it runs through where Pennsylvania, New Jersey, and a small part of New York meet. To get there we travel through vast state parks, densely wooded areas, rustic neighborhoods, and scenic farmland. I love this river, which cuts through the Appalachian Mountains and cruises right on down to Philadelphia. As my friends and I started to get driver's licenses, the draw for many of us was to be able to go explore and have fun out in the Gap. We'd drift down the wide cool river in makeshift tubes and drink beer, linking our arms to make a chain and stopping along the way to explore or get in some kind of

mischief. I've done my share of that. It's also a hotbed for fishing, hiking, and exploring, an outdoor person's heaven.

Out in these woods and alongside this river is where I fell in love with cooking out in nature. From little day trips hiking with friends to cooking in campgrounds and overnights next to the riverbed, I honed the craft. I adapted my skills and knowledge from the kitchen to make use of nature, while refamiliarizing myself with the basics of cooking. But it's a lot of work. You have to pack everything you need, pile it on your back, and head into the woods. It gets heavy and cumbersome, so really think about your essential supplies and tighten it up!

When I bring friends out to the Gap to cook and hang out, we don't bring potato rolls, American cheese, and hamburgers. I'm not judging, as I've certainly cooked my fair share of those American backyard classics. But I challenge you not to rely on the same go-to things you've cooked outdoors before. Consider instead how you'd cook a version of the dishes you cook at home. Don't be afraid! Take a risk. I've brought lobster, ceviche, lamb shanks, whole fish, and all the fruits and veggies to go with them. The key is to create a menu that you can prep in advance and have ready before you leave the house.

Cold morning walk to the river

One of my favorite
swimming holes in
Pennsylvania

Over time, you will get better at the planning and may even adapt your gear and ingredients to the situation. Little tricks that you pick up as you go will help smooth out the experience for you, the cook. It would take a whole book to explain everything I've learned over decades of doing this, and honestly, many of those adaptations might be specific to me. But here are some useful tips to help you get started:

- Invest in a sous vide immersion circulator. Sous vide (or SV as I call it) is the technique of cooking food submerged in hot circulating water. Sealed in a bag with whatever seasoning and flavors you choose, it's the ultimate temperature control and "set it and forget it" style of cooking. Cook it at home a day ahead and let sit in the fridge in the vacuum-sealed bag. It will be perfectly cooked, easy to transport, and ready to crisp up over an open fire! One of my favorite things to cook out in the woods is SV ribs (page 282) or lamb shank: Pre-cooked, packed easily, and no mess. This cooking method is a hero.

- As for cooking fruits and veggies, you can make that as complicated as you want. Get some nice potatoes, stone fruits, spring onions, or whatever is beautiful at the market. I like to cook with the produce that might be growing in the area during that season. Cooking outdoors is a great way to connect you to the season while providing a fresh new experience.

- I freeze broths and use them as ice packs for the hike because when you're hiking and carrying your kitchen and supplies on your back, the weight starts to get serious. Consider using flatbread dough that's frozen or proofing during the hike, to help keep the other ingredients cool. It can then be easily prepped and eaten. That's a 2-for-1 deal, plus a lighter load on the return trip!

- I'm a big guy, and I probably have some pack mule in me. I can carry big packs with cast iron and wire racks along with pounds of food. But having good friends who can help with the heavy lifting is definitely recommended. Distribute the duties! Remember, everyone will enjoy a big payoff at the end.

This chapter is close to my heart, and its true goal is to inspire folks to cook outside. I encourage you to feel confident and capable, to take culinary risks and try to make food an activity to share with the people you love, where you love. But there are a few serious considerations I need to bring to your attention, before you run off to take a dip in the river or wash the smoke off your face. Seriously, please keep the following in mind:

- Cooking in the woods is hard work. Nothing is easy, not even washing your hands or cleaning the dishes. I get that, but one thing I never do is dump my garbage and food waste in the woods and river systems. If it isn't a fish skeleton that I caught from that river, I'm not throwing it into the water. Some may argue that organic food matter will help feed the ecosystem, but leaving things behind is not my style. I left the comforts and ease of a modern indoor kitchen to come and cook in pure nature, in fact I worked my ass off to get here. So, I don't want to see your mess and I'll never leave any mess for you. It goes beyond common courtesy. It's respect for nature.

- Making a fire in the woods can be dangerous. Wildfires are real and sadly many of our friends out West can attest to that. Only make a fire in a place where it makes sense. Check local campgrounds and use designated fire pits or grills. Check to see if ole Smokey the Bear thinks it's a bad idea at the time, and if it is, do something else. Additionally, you *must* have a plan in case things go wrong. Always have a bucket of water nearby to quench the fire quickly and consider how you will react if things go from fun to fucked.

- The areas by the Gap I'm talking about are filled with stories of how people have injured themselves or even died. My dad used to tell a story about a group of teens that went cliff jumping. They'd done it before and thought the water was clear and deep enough. But one kid jumped and landed on a pitchfork that was lodged upright in the muddy bottom. That story scared the hell out of us, and man, how tragic is that. Seriously, you or your friends could get extremely hurt or even killed if you act without caution—especially if you're drinking beer, jumping around, and swimming.

- Stop for a second and think about how the hell you'd get out of the woods with a broken leg. Carrying hurt people out of the woods is dangerous, and the people helping you could get hurt too. It happens all the time. Realistically, you'd probably call the cops who will reach out to a local volunteer rescue team with the know-how to rescue your broken stupid ass. If you're okay, you'll probably end up getting ticketed for trespassing. At best it would be a total waste of a lot of really nice people's time.

- This all comes from a place of love as I've been the stupid person before. I was just lucky enough that I didn't get hurt. Please act with caution and don't be stupid.

The point of this chapter is not to chronicle one specific experience at the Gap. Instead it's a call to action. A call for everyone to get out there and be mindful of where you are and what you are doing. Please help me preserve what I grew up with and value so much. Help me make sure it's there for my boys. I've seen beautiful places with public access get shut down because people acted foolishly. I've also seen places like the ones I'm showing in this book wind up covered in garbage, where my friends and I have literally carried out contractor bags full of trash. If one person reads this chapter and addresses the issues I've outlined, then the time spent sharing a special place and time in my life is worth it.

Be safe, kids, and have some fun cooking outside while you explore this amazing area.

When the air is colder than the water

Sous Vide Mountain Ribs

Makes 1 rack of ribs, about 4 servings

What I love most about this recipe is how easy it is to pull off without compromising flavor or texture. Sous vide is a great way to cook food for eating on a hike in the woods. You do the hard part ahead of time at home, where life is easy, and finish the perfectly cooked ribs over the fire in the woods. It also works well if you're having a dinner party at home: Since most of the prep is done ahead, you won't have to "work" the whole time.

People, including myself, have struggled with making perfect ribs—ribs that don't fall apart in your hands but are still very tender and juicy. By cooking the ribs sous vide, submerged in water and bathed in sauce, the meat will never overcook, but the connective tissues that make meat tough will break down and become tender.

1	**rack pork ribs**, any style, cut in half
1/4 cup	**fermented black bean sauce**
1/4 cup	**sesame oil**
3 Tbsps.	**soy sauce** (I used shoyu)
2 Tbsps.	**honey**
3	**garlic** cloves, grated
2	**scallions**, sliced
1	**Fresno chile**, crushed
2 tsps.	**Pepper Mix** (page 285)
1 tsp.	grated fresh ginger

Throw **all the ingredients** in a vacuum bag and vacuum seal it closed. Preheat a sous vide cooker to keep your water bath at 165°F. Place the bag in the water and cook for 4 hours. The ribs will be perfectly cooked and ready to blast on the grill.

Once the ribs have cooked in the vac bag, they can stay in the fridge for at least a week (and I may have been known to let them go for a couple).

When ready to eat the ribs, remove them from the bag and place on a hot grill or over a fire until they're hot and charred, about 15 minutes. Save the sauce from the bag, which will be nice and fatty and sweet. I like to brush this over the ribs while they reheat and char.

Quick Steaks

Makes as much as you like

If you like to eat meat, then you likely know the cuts such as rib eye, skirt, strip, chop, etc. But try cooking cuts other than the fancier cuts you find in the grocery store. Small cuts of meat often have huge flavor but don't take 45 minutes to rest and cook—items like boneless short rib, minute steaks, and cutlets. You could buy a pork shoulder or sirloin and cut thin small strips, rub and salt them, and cook them quickly. Or explore a local butcher shop and make some good old in-person human relationships. Ask your butcher for some cool ideas—they will have them! And beyond making steaks, alternative cuts are great to cook in stir fries, to use in sandwiches, and to marinate and eat over rice or salad, cold.

small alternative cuts of any
    meat: beef, lamb, pork,
    or venison—whatever you
    want to eat
kosher salt, to taste
Pepper Mix (recipe follows), to
    taste

Slice up your cuts of meat and turn them into little cutlets. Season the meat with salt and pepper mix ahead of time, always. And then just blast 'em off on a hot grill or cast-iron pan—anywhere you've got a heat source and good ventilation.

Pepper Mix

Makes as much as you like

This is a super-easy—but more than satisfying—way to add a little something extra to the situations where you might turn to regular old pepper. The pink and the black peppercorns together give you a warm and fruity, floral aroma and flavor.

I tend to use this on meat *after* I sear it; if you use it before searing, the pepper can burn and become bitter. But sometimes I like that taste! I've eaten plenty of steaks both ways with a smile.

whole black peppercorns
whole pink peppercorns

Add equal parts black and pink peppercorns to a spice mill or the bowl of a mortar and pestle and grind to your desired fineness. Store the ground pepper in a little jar, using a pinch whenever you need it. I make this in little batches, and use it often—the fresher the better.

Fire Prawns

Serves 2

Just because you're a mile into the woods doesn't mean you have to cook just hot dogs and marshmallows. For this recipe I like to get whole head-on prawns, as I love the way the shells get crispy and allow the shrimp to stay juicy and steam in their own juices. I've also done this recipe with unhappy farmed and frozen shrimp…and it works just fine. But when you can, get the best shrimp possible.

Cooking in the woods on wire resting racks is amazing. The racks are super light to pack and they have tiny holes so you won't lose food to the flame gods. The racks also allow for direct dry heat from the fire, and the smoke will kiss the outside of your food.

1/4 cup	gochujang
2 Tbsps.	mirin
2 Tbsps.	sesame oil
2	garlic cloves, grated
1	scallion, thinly sliced
	kosher salt, to taste
	Pepper Mix (page 285), to taste
6	extra-large prawns, shells and heads on

Mix all the ingredients together in a medium bowl or resealable bag and let the shrimp marinate, chilled, for an hour or overnight.

Prepare a medium-hot fire. I place the shrimp on a wire rack about 6 inches above the coals. Cook the shrimp, turning them often to prevent burning, though you do want to get a nice char on the shell. The shrimp should be easy to peel and have snappy white meat in 5 to 10 minutes.

Miso, Cabbage,

Serves 6

This is an easy way to celebrate and enhance one of my favorite vegetables, one of the most important plants ever in the world, the cabbage. And because cabbage and cucumbers are available anytime, you'll have this banger of a recipe in your pocket all year long.

and Cukes

1	small head **cabbage** (red or green), quartered
	kosher salt
2	Persian **cucumbers**
1/2 cup	mixed **nuts and seeds**
2 Tbsps.	salted **butter**
1/4 cup	**white miso**
3 Tbsps.	**extra-virgin olive oil**
2 Tbsps.	**rice vinegar**
	Pepper Mix (page 285), to taste
	mixed **herbs**, optional
	Mountain Spoon Sauce (next page), optional

Over a hot fire, char the cabbage quarters on all sides then season with salt. Cook the cucumbers whole over super-high heat so that the outsides char but the insides are still cool and crunchy. Toast the nuts and seeds in a small skillet and then chop them coarsely.

Cut the cukes and cabbage into bite-size pieces and place in a large bowl. In a saucepan, melt the butter, miso, and olive oil together. (Leave the butter at room temp while cooking the cabbage to really help this process along.) Drizzle the miso mixture over the cukes and cabbage and toss to coat.

Add the toasted nuts and seeds, the vinegar, pepper mix, and herbs (if using) and mix well until everything is coated evenly. Top with some mountain spoon sauce if you want, but it's not required!

Mountain Spoon Sauce

1 cup	kimchi, chopped
1/2 cup	juice from kimchi
1/2 cup	extra-virgin olive oil
	juice of 1/2 lemon
1 Tbsp.	honey
1/2 cup	mixed herb leaves, such as parsley, cilantro, etc.
1	scallion, thinly sliced
1 Tbsp.	sesame seeds
1 Tbsp.	mixed grated garlic and fresh ginger
1 tsp.	red pepper flakes

Makes 1 pint

This sauce is delicious on almost anything (like most spoon sauces), with a nice and funky kimchi kick to it. Adding the kimchi juice is an easy way to get an umami blast even in the middle of the woods. I put the sauce on anything off the grill or fire; it's spicy and funky with nuttiness from sesame and a hint of sweetness.

Place **all the ingredients** in a quart jar and screw the lid on tight, then shake it until you no longer want to anymore. Or you can whisk the ingredients together in a bowl.

I also like to add the kimchi juice, lemon juice, and honey to a blender and slowly pour in the oil with the blender running to form an emulsification. Then I fold in the remaining ingredients and store it in a jar for a few days.

Herbed Flatbread

Makes 1 flatbread

When you're grilling in the woods you might just need a warm flatbread to use as a plate. Plus, dough is smaller to pack than the bread it becomes—yes, that sounds ridiculous, but you'll see. Scale this recipe up for as many people as you have to feed.

1 ball	Brad's Sourdough (page 153)
	extra-virgin olive oil
	kosher salt
	ground black pepper
1 Tbsp.	salted butter
1/4 cup	mixed fresh herbs
	firm cheese of choice, thinly shaved
	pickled onions

Shape the dough to your desired size and place it in a heated cast-iron pan or on a wire rack over a hot fire. Cook each side and flip/move as needed so it doesn't burn. Once the amount of color you want is achieved, move the bread to a cooler area to let the bread bake through.

Top the bread with the remaining ingredients and let the cheese melt a bit before serving. I like to cut the bread into pieces and let people grab and eat!

Deer Dad

Sussex County, Northern New Jersey
Late Autumn

12

My dad loves to hunt. From deer to turkey, it's a part of him and something he's done since he was a boy. His interest and commitment were a subcurrent and consistent theme in our household, shaping memories, providing a specialized education, and allowing for quality time together.

Dad worked two jobs for pretty much my whole life and free time was tight. But, early weekend mornings in season were for hunting, and some evenings were for preparing. My sister and I were always included in his interests, and we were taught from the youngest age how and why hunting was important. Bow hunting was his favorite. Even as a small boy I was intrigued and excited to watch and learn. Inevitably, I too fell in love with archery and the outdoors.

Being outside and tuned into nature was what really got me interested (besides wanting to be like my dad). Even as a little guy, too young to join on the actual hunt, I have incredible memories of helping my dad set up tree stands. We'd take scouting walks through the thick woods searching for the perfect tree, a space that was accessible but hidden, with a clear view of the land and what we hoped would be a great spot for deer. Talking and teaching the whole time, my dad would set it up. He was so strong, knowledgeable, and capable: climbing, reinforcing, and planning ahead with a quiet thoughtfulness. He explained it all with patience and consistently reminded me to respect the land and the animal. Once set up, he'd let me sit up in the tree stand and I'd take a moment and pretend to be him, seeing the land through his eyes.

My dad preferred the morning hunt, and the night before heading out he'd get all tuned up and set up; everything laid out on the floor, ready to go before first light. There was anticipation and excitement in the preparation, like a kid on Christmas Eve or the night before a big vacation. He had it set up so the only thing we did in the morning was get dressed, drink coffee, and eat oatmeal. He'd come into my room and wake me up, then start the truck and let it warm up while he prepared his green Stanley thermos. We'd sit in the dark kitchen so as to not wake up the rest of the house.

Outside was just as dark, but cold, always cold. We'd then take an early morning truck ride to a location where we could park, with the heat blasting and radio low. I could look out the window and see the stars, or maybe the moon would give us some light as we walked into the woods as quietly as possible, watching closely for signs of deer before the sun came up. As a kid, I dreaded this part, the early darkness and the cold, but as I grew older I looked forward to it.

Now that I'm an adult, Dad and I follow the same exact routine but once in the woods we set a time to meet back up, and we each have our own tree stands. You have to be quiet and careful as you climb 20 feet up in the tree, pulling your bow and gear up as you settle into your stand. Since all the preparations are done ahead of time, you can take comfort in knowing you're in good shape. You're among animals that you've come to know, having studied them for months. It's their home and you're visiting.

The name of the game is: Do not move, sit in the cold tree, and do not move. Ha—great for kids! My sister hated it and didn't last long in the hunting world. But if you can get past the early mornings and let the cold and the quiet wrap around you as the light cracks the horizon and starts to creep through the still forest, you begin to notice the detail. All your senses become heightened. Songbirds break the silence and sunlight washes over the ground cover,

Getting some arrows
in while the sausages
smoke

squirrels scurry down the oak trees and dart across the forest floor. You might see an owl swoop by or a fox lurk in the distance; he probably senses you. But I've seen hawks land 5 feet from me and never realize I was there. Coyotes have come trotting down the path through the thicket, where I'd hoped deer would be, but the coyotes are cool to see too. I look forward to seeing the woods come to life. Whether it's therapeutic or generally good for modern humans, I don't know, but I do think everyone should experience it at some point.

While all of that is happening, every single noise you hear, you think is a deer. You're on high alert and the anticipation is palpable. Every now and then on a lucky or well-planned day, that little crunch to the side of you which has been Sammy the squirrel all morning is a big whitetail deer! The excitement kicks in. But you're also worried that the deer is going to hear your heart beating with excitement. Your breathing falls into a slow pattern bringing you into an almost Zen calm; you don't even blink an eye. It's amazing how in tune deer are to the environment, so you have to be in tune with it too. The first thing they do is smell you, because let's be honest, humans stink. Their keen hearing will then pinpoint you; those ears are like sonar pivoting around and picking up the slightest sound.

Deer do two things well: Eat and try not to get eaten. That's why I love bow hunting the most, you need to be so close and in tune with the animal. Even then you still might blow it from time to time; it's hard and I love that. I have no problem hunting with a rifle or other means if you can get a clean shot. But my dad taught me to never

shoot unless I am confident it will result in a clean, quick, and compassionate death. I'll wait till the next time if I don't have a clean shot, and I hope you do the same.

Losing animals you shoot in the woods is a reality that isn't often talked about. In nature, nothing goes to waste, and a deer you shoot and lose will be eaten from meat to bones by other animals. The point is that the animal's life should not be taken for granted, it should be valued and appreciated. And they should never suffer.

My dad practiced with his bow shooting targets in the yard. About 20 yards into hay bales, a nice and safe little system. Us kids would sit on the back deck and watch before dinner. Dad has never shot a deer over 25 yards with the bow. But as I got back into archery, I began to enjoy shooting arrows at longer distances, 60 to 120 yards. For me, it's about discipline, patience, and mental strength. Long distance hunting is not my intent; instead the long distance is for target shooting and honing my skills.

The bows we shoot have a sight system with a pin that you use to place the arrows on a target. So one day I asked my dad why he doesn't shoot further than 30 yards, even when practicing. He simply said, "Why the hell would I wanna do that?" I can't help but respect that as a hunter and human. I did finally get him to start shooting longer distances with me, and now he likes to fling them far for fun. My teenage niece got into archery too—she's target-only right now and goes to lessons and competes. Dad sure is excited about this, buying her a nice compound bow. Bow and arrow demands mental skill and acuity, and is a great sport for the whole family.

My dad has harvested deer every year since I can remember, and I'm grateful for having access to venison meat throughout my life. You can tell venison is different from the meat you get at the store simply by the color, which is a deep purplish red. Deer are a rather lean animal with almost no intermuscular fat. "Less is more" when it comes to preparing it. Salt the venison ahead of time and sure as hell don't overcook it! Avoid hammering it with heat, as it can quickly turn to leather on you.

Stews and roasts are a great choice and were my mom's go to techniques.

Two of the recipes I share in this chapter are close to my heart and something I will pass on to my boys: venison sausages and backstrap steak and eggs. They're easy to make, delicious, and extremely approachable to folks who haven't dabbled much with game meat. Cooking venison could be a book of its own—maybe I'll do that one day. For now, I want these stories to get you to try new foods and know what goes into hunting deer. Whether you get out there yourself is up to you. If not, maybe you know someone who has venison to share. I bet if you asked around, you could find some.

Hunting deer is a tradition my dad bonded over with his dad, and something he then taught me. Today, it gets me out into nature, and also prods me to take on an active conservationist role while providing high-quality food for my family.

I talk about my family a lot in this book; I find it hard not to. I was lucky to be born into a loving family and I believe it's important to recognize and appreciate that. After all, their influence shaped me into the adult I am. Yes, Dad taught me to hunt, but it was much more than that. He instilled in me a deep respect for nature and the animal itself; you never kill an animal unless you are going to eat it. He always said that with such a serious tone that I had no choice but to hear him. I'm so grateful for that lesson. You can spend a lot of money on gear and guides, but what you can't buy is class, respect, and love. Honoring the land, appreciating the moment, and respecting animals and the planet is what matters most.

I've also grown to love the rituals; shooting and killing an animal is only a small fraction of what hunting really is. I didn't get a deer this year. I saw a bunch but didn't feel like I had a good shot. Did I get out into the stand enough and put all the work in during the off-season? No, but my dad and some buddies sure did. I went into the woods grateful to spend time with them.

And even though I didn't get a deer myself, I still got some meat in the freezer. It's funny how hunters are so eager to share something that they've worked so hard for. I love that and look forward to returning the kindness…hopefully next season.

Cabbage Kraut

Makes about 2 quarts

The dead stuff you buy in a bag just isn't going to do it anymore. Make your own raw sauerkraut instead.

2	small heads cabbage
	kosher salt, 2 percent of the weight of the cleaned cut cabbage (see Notes on Fermentation, page 42)
8	garlic cloves, chopped
1 tsp.	pink peppercorns, crushed
	additional spices (optional and up to you)

This is a very simple recipe with very few ingredients, so get the best stuff you can as it will really come through in the final product. Always try to get organic when fermenting, as residual pesticides and such can inhibit the fermentation process.

Start by coring the cabbage and slicing it into 1/4-inch shreds. That thickness is completely changeable and just my personal preference.

Next, add the shredded cabbage to a large bowl and add the salt. Mix and massage the cabbage for about 20 minutes or more, using your hands to bruise and gently crush the

Continues on
next page

cabbage with the salt to draw out moisture. This salty liquid will be the brine for the sauerkraut.

Once a good pool of brine has formed, mix in the garlic, peppercorns, and spices. Mix thoroughly and taste the batch before letting it ferment. If it seems overly salty, add more cabbage, or add more salt if it tastes underseasoned.

Transfer the cabbage mixture to a crock or large inert vessel, and pack it down so all of the cabbage mixture is under the brine. You can use a weight or a bag of rocks if needed to keep it submerged. Cover with a clean towel or cheesecloth and secure it with a rubber band, then let ferment at room temperature in a dark spot of the house for at least a week. It will start to get bubbly, the color will become muted, and the cabbage strips will become softer and will produce a lot of liquid. Check on it every day or two to ensure that the kraut is submerged under the brine. When it's funky enough for you, store it in the fridge indefinitely.

Party boat picture

Brad's Spicy Mustard

Makes 1 pint

Once you see how simple this is to make, you might never buy prepared mustard again. It's such an easy condiment to make at home and get better at, figuring out over time the nuances of making a really subtle mature mustard. It's a classic house staple that's fun to make and experiment with, and great with my dad's kielbasa (page 312).

6 Tbsps.	brown mustard seeds
5 Tbsps.	yellow mustard seeds
1 Tbsp.	mustard powder
1/2 cup	verjus or white wine
1/4 cup	apple cider vinegar
1/4 cup	kraut juice (optional)
1 Tbsp.	kosher salt

Mix both mustard seeds and the mustard powder together and blend or grind using a spice mill or mortar and pestle into the consistency you desire in a mustard. This will be the texture control.

Once blended and ground, add the verjus, vinegar, kraut juice (if using), and salt and mix thoroughly. Don't be alarmed if it's very loose and soupy and looks nothing like mustard at first. It will thicken as the seeds and powder hydrate. If it looks too thick, add a splash of water or wine.

I let my mustard ferment in a cloth-covered jar at room temperature for about a week, then I allow it to age in the fridge for a few days. I feel it helps develop flavor and tame the bitterness. The fermentation is not mandatory in a rush, but maybe we should all slow down a bit.

Now you have some amazing mustard that can store in the fridge for quite some time—if it lasts!

Breakfast Steak, Eggs, and Potatoes

Serves 2

When I was young and my dad got a deer, the treat I remember most was the backstrap steak and eggs, along with potatoes or some toast. Man, it was so good and so different. It was how I fell in love with venison. Hope you make this one at home. If you can get your hands on a backstrap of venison from hunting or a friend who does, I guarantee it will be the best steak and eggs to date!

8 ounces	venison backstrap (or any favorite small cut of red meat)
	kosher salt, to taste
2	large Idaho potatoes, peeled
1	shallot, peeled
	olive oil or animal fat
	pinch of cayenne
4	eggs
	freshly ground black pepper, to taste

Salt your meat at least an hour before cooking. While that's happening, grate the potatoes and the shallot into a bowl lined with a cloth towel.

Add 1 teaspoon salt and mix thoroughly. Massage the potatoes every few minutes so the salt can draw out the moisture. We do this because we want the potatoes to be crispy, and if they're soaked with liquid that will never happen.

After about 20 minutes of salt massaging, squeeze the potato-onion mixture using the

Continues on next page

Continued
from previous
page

rag to bring out the water. Do this harder than you might think you need to: The drier you get the potatoes, the better! Mix in the pinch of cayenne.

When ready to cook, preheat a cast-iron pan with some oil or animal fat over medium heat. I make one big potato pancake in the skillet by using my fingers to pack the mixture into the pan. Form it tight and the potato starch should bind it all together beautifully.

Depending on the size of your pan and potatoes, this should take 15 to 20 minutes total; flip the potato disc once halfway through. If it's sticking you can add a little more fat and remember most people's first attempt at potato pancakes usually isn't the best. Be patient and don't force the flip. Like cooking fish, the bottom of the potatoes will release when ready. Let the crispy potatoes rest on a wire rack when done.

As for the steak and the eggs, just cook them the way you love. I love my steak cooked in cast iron to medium, with a little pepper added at the end. My eggs? Fried over medium in olive oil.

Dry-aged whitetail deer in a
walk-in refrigerator

Dad's Recipes

The following recipes come from my dad. They're just as my old man gave them to me, and that's how I'm giving them to you. This style of recipe is enough to get you inspired, enough to get it done. There might be a few gaps, but you'll figure it out. The idea is to evolve these into your own family recipes. You're going to want to change it over time, and I want you to.

These recipes were my first experience with making sausage other than sweet Italian varieties. While my dad grew up in Jersey, he had a love for Cajun ingredients and cooking. I remember how he always said that andouille wasn't just a sausage, it was an ingredient all on its own. As he explored his cooking practices, he started folding in local venison meat to Cajun recipes and came up with some riffs of his own. To me, that's what cooking is all about.

Andouille Sausage   Pork or 1/2 pork 1/2 venison

- 5 lb meat ground a little coarse (grind meat very cold semi froz)
- 5 tsp Black pepper
- 2 table kosher salt
- 4 tsp red pepper
- 8-10 cloves garlic fine dice
- 1 tsp curing salt.
- 1/2 cup red wine optional
- mix everything - your hands work best
- put in frig over nite
- pork casing 35 -38 mm.
- before stuffing cases mix meat mixture with 3/4 cup ice water
- after stuffed let sausage air dry for 1 hr.
- smoke 4 hr @ 160-180° internal temp hits 150°.
- root beer or birch beer in bottom pan adds nice flavor.
- when done drop sausage in ice water bath, 10 min, then let finish cooling out of water,
- it'll last few days in frig · freezes well when vacum packed.

pork and venison keilbasa.

- 5lb pork butt
- 5 lb venion
- pork easing 35-38 mm.
- tea pink curing salt
- 1 table marjoram
- 3-5 cloves garlic fine dice
- 1cup powder milk
- 2 table black pepper.
- mix all spices
- cut meat in strips then semi freeze (meat grinds better that way)
- grind meat hot real fine - mix well and add about cup and 1/2 of ice water.
- stuff casings - and let air dry about 1 hr.
- then smoke 180-185. about 3 hr. 150° internal temp
- when done put keilbasa in ice water bath. to
- cool about 10 min - this shocks and stops cooking when fully cooled vacum pack and freeze.

Jambalaya.

- 1/2 lb. keilbasa or Anduillie sliced
- 2 chicken breast bite size pieces
- 1-lb shrimp
- 1 cup green pepper, onion, celery fine dice
- 1 cup " " " " bite size pieces
- 3-4 bay leaves.
- 1 large can diced tomatos plus 1/2 can paste
- 2 cups Rice
- 1 tea red pepper. black pepper, salt, tyme, oregano. mix

- brown sausage in olive oil with bay leaves and spices on high Heat always scraping bottom. 5 mi
- then add fine dice veggies. 10 min scrape bottom.
- then add rest of veggie 10 mins " "
- add tomato and paste mix well scrape bottom.
- add chicken 10 min scrape bottom.
- peel shrimp and boil skins 3 1/2 cups water for stock
※ do this ahead of time
- add dry rice stir in for couple min add shrimp stock lower Heat 15 min add shrimp. When rice is done ready more hot sauce can be added to taste,

My Love for the Cold

13

Pristine beaches, storied fishing docks, iconic lighthouses, and world-class surfing bring thousands of visitors to Montauk, New York, every summer. The farthest Long Island beach point from Manhattan, Montauk juts out into the Atlantic and is no secret to those in the Northeast.

For decades, this quiet hamlet has been a destination for cool kids, artisans, and the super wealthy. A decrepit, decommissioned military base, Camp Hero, takes up some prime real estate. There's a park surrounding the grounds, which have been the subject of conspiracy theories and bygone military missions likened to James Bond movies. "No Trespassing" signs add to the mystique.

As a kid, my family stuck to points down the Jersey shore, and never ventured out this way. It wasn't until my mid-twenties, when I was in culinary school and living in New York City, that I began to explore this area. Really, my buddies and I were just chasing waves, and Montauk is a sweet surf spot. Since then, I've had some of the best times of my life here, cooking with friends and generally doing really cool shit.

In the late summer and early fall, the weather is perfect, the water is clear and warm, striped bass roll their fat bodies right up onto the beach, and there's always a surf swell somewhere. The problem is that everyone goes there then, and during the peak season there's just not the same vibe you find in the off-season.

I'm sure some locals will lump me into the flood of annoying city traffic that overwhelms the town on summer weekends, and maybe they're not wrong. But I've seen some summer visitors totally trash the place, leaving garbage all over the beach, flooding their $130,000 SUV engines while illegally driving on the beach, and leaving vodka seltzer cans roadside. I guess that could be said about any cool beach town these days, though, huh?

I have really come to enjoy Montauk in the winter. I'm talking the dead of February, when it's 21°F and the wind chaps your face, where there are no crowds of people getting drunk and leaving messes. Driving out in that weather to a seasonally abandoned town where 80 percent of the stores and restaurants are closed might not

seem worth it. But I'm also not the only one who loves the off-season. Plenty of folks do live out east all year long and appreciate the beauty of Montauk in the winter.

I feel that in a way, the Northeastern cold temperatures act as a purifier, cleaning the air and water, snapping you awake and reminding you of the power and majesty of the seasons. I don't remember where I heard this, but there's a saying that goes, "There's no such thing as bad weather, just bad gear." Even in the winter, there are surfers (who are way better than me) in the freezing ocean, cranking on gorgeous waves. It's not always freezing, obviously, but the water is damn cold and wearing the right wetsuit is mandatory unless you want to face hypothermia. Having to purchase and then don a thick wetsuit keeps a lot of people away, but when the waves are good, surfers will do what they have to.

I try to make an annual winter trip to Montauk. We get an off-season rental, and when we arrive get a little fire going in the wood stove and prep a nice hot meal. The cold winter nights bring out some incredible stars.

I plan all my home-cooked meal prep before arriving, since most businesses are closed. Set yourself up so that the days and nights flow nicely. Bring some cool cuts of meat and ingredients that will recharge the body and mind. These cold winter days are perfect for everyone to cook long format recipes or start a nice food project. If you're out hiking or trying to surf in ice cold water, you'll be burning some calories. A delicious and nutritious meal after a day like that is only matched by a nice hot shower.

Pat, Kenyon, and I had big plans to catch some waves ourselves and get some food and surfing pictures in, too. In my head, I imagined a picturesque light snow while I cranked down a wave…real cool stuff. Well, it was cold all right…stupid cold, with temps in the low teens. Kenyon said it was the coldest he'd ever been in his life, and I was the one in the damn water! Actually, the gear and technology I had in my winter wetsuit might've left me warmer than him, plus I was out paddling around… while Kenyon and Pat stood on the beach for an hour and a half taking pictures of me and the waves. Sorry, guys.

The snow never showed up and the waves were few and far between. Even worse, the two waves that I should have ripped on, I absolutely blew. I was pissed at myself for months after that. I really wanted that iconic picture of me riding a wave (which I swear, I've totally done) in the closing chapter of this book. Sure, there are a million pictures of people way better than me surfing perfect waves, but I had hoped to capture that moment for myself. That's life. Still, I was pretty lucky to be surfing and cooking food with my buddies out in Montauk!

The real point of this chapter isn't about catching a perfect wave. It's that everyone who can ought to try to enjoy nature and cooking in the cold seasons of the Northeast. The season, landscape, and comfort food go so well together. Dig into big rich braises and soups, hearty stocks, and winter salads. You have the extra time to cook when you're hunkered in the house and it gets dark at 4:45 p.m.

If you are lucky enough to catch some snow while doing all of this, you're living the dream. I'll hold out hope for next year's Montauk trip—and since no one will be taking pictures of me then, I'm sure I'll surf a hell of a lot better and finally catch that big wave. And when I head to the kitchen after a cold day outside, it'll be full of hearty, home-cooked foods stewing and simmering away.

An empty Ditch Plains parking lot. Something you will not see in the summer.

This picture stings. On a day that was zero degrees and you had to work for waves, I truly blew standing up on this one.

Braised Lamb Shanks

Makes 3 servings

A nicely braised lamb shank is satisfying
after being in the cold weather—not only
is it hot and filling, but it's gelatinous and
nourishing too. And the little salty zingy
hot olives in here? I'm always a fan. It's
easy to cozy up next to the fire with this.

3	lamb shanks
	kosher salt
1/4 cup	extra-virgin olive oil
1 cup	white wine
2 cups	canned crushed tomatoes
1/4 cup	honey
8	garlic cloves, peeled, crushed, and chopped
1	cinnamon stick
1 Tbsp.	red pepper flakes
1/4 tsp.	ground coriander
10	shallots, peeled and sliced
2 pounds	rutabagas, turnips, and/or golden beets, scrubbed or peeled and cut into chunks
1 cup	pitted green olives

Rub the shanks with salt and refrigerate for 24 hours before cooking.

Preheat the oven to 250°F. Pat the shanks dry. Heat the oil in a heavy ovenproof skillet or Dutch oven and sear the shanks on all sides.

Add the wine, tomatoes, honey, garlic, cinnamon stick, pepper flakes, and coriander to the shanks. Roast, covered, until the meat is nice and tender but not falling off the bone, about 2 1/2 hours.

Raise the oven temperature to 400°F and remove the lid. Add the shallots, rutabagas, and olives and stir well. I like to have as much of the meat poking out of the liquid at this point so it browns. Place back in the oven and blast for 15 to 30 minutes, until the exposed meat darkens but doesn't burn. Watch it!

Winter

Salad

6 to 8	baby bok choy, chopped
1 head	radicchio, torn or chopped
1	avocado, sliced or diced

Dressing

1/4 cup	extra-virgin olive oil
	juice of 2 lemons
1 Tbsp.	honey
	generous amount of Brad's Za'atar (page 227) or store-bought
	kosher salt

Makes about 6 servings

This salad is super simple and easy to shop for, and very friendly to the addition of your favorite protein or fruits and nuts. I developed the recipe one night to serve with the lamb shanks just before this.

Place the bok choy, radicchio, and avocado in a large bowl. Whisk the dressing ingredients together in a small mixing bowl. Drizzle it over the vegetables and avocado and toss to coat. Season to taste and serve.

Big

Stock

This stock will save your life and the ones you love! Drink it straight as a morning elixir or use it as the base for soup. Making stock is one of my favorite things to do in the world of cooking. It nourishes the soul and is one of the foods I find myself craving in a deep, primal way. Gelatinous to the point it makes your lips sticky and solidifies when cold, when made properly, it's a liquid meal on its own.

In my opinion, stock or broth isn't the place to just throw in your half-gone-bad produce. I still try to use the best ingredients I can get, and freeze bones and other animal parts throughout the months to defrost when I want to make stock. Knuckle or joint bones make the best sticky broths. I like to add a smoked ham hock to the mix to give a mild smoky flavor as well as a big gelatin boost.

In addition to bones, I also like to freeze mushroom stems to use for stock making. There are lots of different broths and stocks out there with all types of names and ingredients. I haven't found a version I can't get into.

1/4 cup	extra-virgin olive oil
3	medium onions, halved
	handful mixed mushrooms
2	medium carrots, scrubbed
3	celery stalks
10 pounds	mixed bones (see Notes), roasted or not
1 bunch	parsley
	additional fresh herbs (thyme, lemongrass, rosemary, etc.—dealer's choice)
2 heads	garlic, halved around the equator or left whole
6	bay leaves
1 Tbsp.	whole black peppercorns
1 cup	white wine
4 gallons	filtered water
	kosher salt

In a large pot, heat the oil over medium-high heat and brown off the onions, mushrooms, carrots, and celery until some light caramelization forms. Add the bones, parsley and other herbs, garlic, bay leaves, and peppercorns and stir. Add the wine and let reduce for a few minutes. Add the water and bring to a bare simmer. Turn the heat down

Continues on next page

Continued
from previous
page

to medium low; you want a gentle, light, bubbling simmer, not a roaring boil.

Let this liquid simmer away for hours—all day or even overnight. See Notes for estimates. Taste the stock, watch it, and give it time. Time and low heat will extract the nutrients and wonderful sticky gelatin from the bones. That awesome, lip-smacking sticky feeling you get from your favorite ramen shop comes from the gelatin in a well-made stock.

Once done, remove the pot from the heat and allow the stock to cool a bit. I like to use a large slotted spoon or spider to scoop, drain off, and then discard the large chunks of vegetables and bones. Once the big pieces are gone, pour the stock through a fine-mesh strainer lined with cheesecloth. Season with salt after you are done. Seasoning ahead is doable but opens up the possibility of making the stock too salty once it is reduced.

Use the stock immediately, or store in the fridge for a few days and take what you need when you need it, spooning off any solidified fat that forms on the surface. I love to transfer stock to quart and pint containers and keep it frozen for other nights and days when I need some liquid medicine.

I like a mix of roasted bones—chicken, pork, beef, turkey...but you can certainly just use one type! For beef and pork bones, I'll often blanch them first in a large stockpot filled with cold water. Bring the water to a hard simmer, then turn it to low and cook for 15 minutes. Discard all the water and rinse the bones and meat. Often I'll then coat the bones with a little oil and roast in a 475°F oven until they're toasty and browned, about 20 minutes. This adds depth of flavor and a darker color to the finished stock.

As for timing, big bones and large cuts with lots of connective tissue and cartilage will need to simmer longer than small pieces like chicken wings. As rough guidelines, big beef bones should simmer for 12 to 50 hours; pork bones for 12 to 24 hours; and poultry bones for 6 to 24 hours. When using a mix of bones, I'll often add chicken parts hours after the beef bones. The longer you simmer, the stickier the stock!

An outdoor shower, drying off wetsuits

Mustard-Roasted

Leftover pork? Take some slices or pieces and toss them with some oil. Sear them cut-sides down until a nice crispy crust forms. Use to make some quick tacos, or serve the crispy pork with some fermented veggies or pickles you might have in the fridge and you're set for the next day's dinner. Or pull some stock from the freezer and make ramen (page 334). I love me some quality leftovers.

Pork
Shoulder

Serves 6

Go ahead and use the mustard you made on page 304, or one that's been lurking in the fridge for a while. This is a simple way to make a great dinner or meal anytime.

4 pounds	boneless pork shoulder, or 7 pounds bone-in shoulder
	kosher salt
1/2 cup	Dijon mustard
2 Tbsps.	mirin
2 Tbsps.	shoyu
2 Tbsps.	Pepper Mix (page 285)
	minced fresh chile (optional for heat)
1/4 cup	extra-virgin olive oil
6	small sweet potatoes
	cloves from 1 head garlic, crushed and peeled
2 to 3	bunches mustard greens, torn

Rub the pork with as much salt as you can get to stick to the meat, wrap it in plastic, and refrigerate for about 24 hours before cooking. (The meat can go 12 hours or up to 48 hours, depending on your schedule.)

Preheat the oven to 250°F. Mix the mustard, mirin, shoyu, pepper mix, and chile in a bowl. Rub the mixture all over the pork. Place the oil, pork, sweet potatoes, and garlic in a large Dutch oven or roasting pan and place on the middle rack of the oven. Roast for 2 hours. Increase the oven temperature to 300°F and roast for 1 more hour.

Turn the heat up to 400 or 425°F and blast the meat for 8 to 12 minutes, until it gets nice, crispy, and caramelized. Keep an eye on it here as it can burn fast. Remove the pan from the oven and start to mound the greens over the potatoes and meat. Stuff them everywhere. Let the meat rest for 20 to 60 minutes like this; the heat from the dish will wilt the greens in a way I love.

Once rested, I slice the meat and place it back over the greens. Season with a little salt if needed. Occasionally I squeeze some lemon over it all, and sprinkle with Za'atar (page 227)! Pork is so easy and welcomes flavor riffing!

Leftover Pork Shoulder

Ramen

Serves 6

I'm a huge soup person. I grew up with my mom's chicken noodle soup, which is one of my favorite things in life, and something I am constantly riffing on. Later, when I was introduced to deeply flavorful and nourishing noodle soups like ramen from Japan, I started experimenting with them, too.

This dish comes together fast and is a perfect way to use leftover meat, like some from the Mustard-Roasted Pork Shoulder (page 332). When the stock is made already and frozen, and the pork has been cooked, the time-consuming parts are done and you can slap together a perfect meal in a few minutes.

extra-virgin olive oil
2 scallions, 1 thickly sliced and 1 thinly sliced
2 mushrooms of your choice, thinly sliced
1 quart Big Stock (page 326)
10 ounces fresh or frozen ramen noodles (the best you can get)
2 slices roast pork shoulder, 1/2 inch thick
1 radish, thinly sliced
6 snow peas, thinly sliced
2 whole egg yolks
handful of greens of your choice, thinly sliced
Brad's Furikake (page 195) or store-bought furikake, to taste

In a medium saucepan, heat a little olive oil over medium-high heat and cook the thickly sliced scallion and the mushrooms until browned a little. Add the frozen or defrosted stock right to the pan and stir well. Bring to a simmer and keep hot.

In a separate pot, cook the ramen noodles according to package directions or to your preference. Meanwhile, place the slices of pork in a hot skillet and sear on one side.

Place a nice bunch of noodles in each of two bowls and ladle some broth in. Place a slice of seared pork down in each bowl and garnish with radish, snow peas, egg yolk, the thinly sliced scallions, and greens. Hit with a little furikake, and you are set!

Roasted Garlic

and

Miso

Butter

Makes about 2 cups

This stuff is just great to have ready in the kitchen, especially in the cold months when room-temperature butter can really last a while on the kitchen counter. From brushing on some fish for roasting to smearing on toast and making your favorite eggs in the AM, you can't go wrong with roasted garlic butter. Freeze any extra, if you like.

Roasted Garlic

2 heads	garlic extra-virgin olive oil kosher salt
1 pound	cultured butter, room temperature
1 Tbsp.	white miso
1/4 cup	chopped parsley Pepper Mix (page 285)

For the roasted garlic: Preheat the oven to 350°F (or wait until you're cooking a dish that requires this oven temperature; I always roast garlic when I'm roasting other items).

Slice the top 1 inch or so off each garlic head with a heavy knife or shears. Nip enough off to expose the tips of the cloves. Drizzle oil over the cut sides so it flows between the exposed tips. Season with a little salt and wrap the heads together in one packet of foil. I like to flick a little water into the foil packet with my finger to help steam and prevent over-caramelization.

Roast the garlic until the cloves are a nice golden color and their texture is creamy and smooth, 1 hour to 1 hour 15 minutes. When the heads are cool enough to handle, remove the garlic by pushing the cloves right out of the papery skins.

Mash the garlic and fold it into the room temperature butter. Mash in the miso and stir in the parsley at the end. Season with salt and pepper. Keep it in the fridge, covered, or in a cool spot in the kitchen for a few days. If you roll it up in wax paper and freeze it, it'll last for a couple months.

Tinned Sardine Toast

with Thin Fennel-Mushroom Salad

Makes about 6 servings

There's a reason everything in the ocean wants to eat sardines—they're good for you, and they're high in nutrients, protein, and oils. They're satisfying fuel, and delicious. Sardines are a rather cheap and available ingredient that you can make a really delicious salad or meal out of. With a little help, they can become a world-class snack or lunch.

2 Tbsps.	extra-virgin olive oil, plus more for drizzling
2 Tbsps.	capers, minced
2 Tbsps.	chopped fresh parsley
1 Tbsp.	mayonnaise
1 tsp.	lemon juice
	kosher salt and Pepper Mix (page 285), to taste
1	small head fennel
6	button mushrooms
	toasted sourdough bread
	salted butter, for smearing
2 (3- to 5-ounce)	tins fish (sardines, mackerel, trout, whatever)

For the dressing, in a medium bowl, whisk together the oil, capers, parsley, mayonnaise, and lemon juice. Season with salt and pepper mix and add more lemon or mayo if you want to adjust the consistency.

Shave the fennel and mushrooms with a mandoline or very sharp knife into very thin slices. Add to the dressing in the bowl and gently toss to coat. Drizzle with a little more oil if needed.

Toast up some nice sourdough you just made or have frozen in the freezer and smear a little butter on the slices. Spoon the dressed salad onto the toast and top with chunks of the fish. Sprinkle with salt and pepper and then drizzle with your finest oil…you're set.

Thanks, Pat

Thank Yous

Huge thanks to Mother Nature for providing. Massive thank you to Peggy, my wife, who made it possible for me to make this book. Pat, for being my good buddy and taking awesome pictures, Uncle Doom, and Kenyon aka Core Strength Craig. Endless thank yous to my parents; my sister, Kristi; Dan; Vinny; James; Evan; Jay; Captain Matt and Tony; Stone Acres Farm; Gerry; John; Javier; Maggie; the Suarez family; Alexander Design; Seacoast Mushrooms; Orvis; Yeti; and Traeger. Thanks to my editor, Mike, and the whole publishing team, including Tracy, Janis, Ben, Nyamekye, Deri, Thea, Jules, Jess, and Lauren. Also big thanks to everyone who has helped, inspired, and supported me over the years, and anyone I happened to forget. I love all of you.

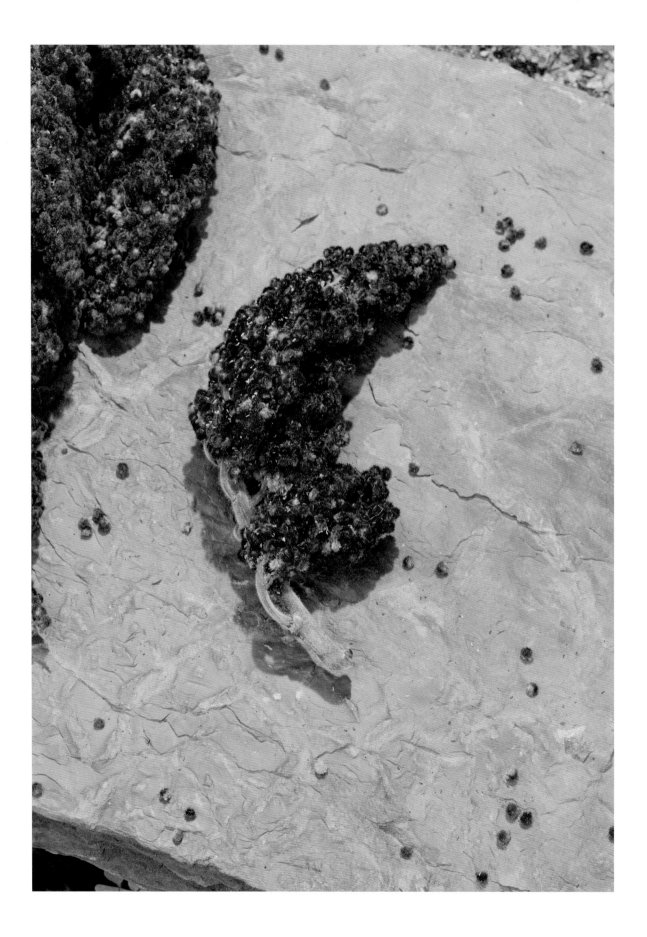

Index

About the Author

Brad Leone is a chef and online video star known for his *Bon Appétit* web series, *It's Alive*. Before joining *Bon Appétit* as a dishwasher and working his way up to test kitchen manager, he was a professional carpenter and attended culinary school. He lives in coastal Connecticut with his wife and sons. This is his first book.

◎ @brad_leone bradleone.com

Voracious / Little, Brown and Company
Hachette Book Group
1290 Avenue of the Americas, New York, NY 10104
littlebrown.com

First Edition: November 2021

Voracious is an imprint of Little, Brown and Company, a division of Hachette Book Group, Inc. The Voracious name and logo are trademarks of Hachette Book Group, Inc.

The publisher is not responsible for websites (or their content) that are not owned by the publisher.

The Hachette Speakers Bureau provides a wide range of authors for speaking events. To find out more, go to hachettespeakersbureau.com or call (866) 376-6591.

Book design by Tracy Ma
Photography by Pat O'Malley
Additional photographs on pages 93 and 107 (top) by Brad Leone

ISBN 978-0-316-49735-0
LCCN 2021936250

10 9 8 7 6 5 4 3 2 1

GRAPHIUS
Printed in Belgium